THE PARK ESTATE, NOTTI[
Ken Brand

1. INTRODUCTION

In May 1795 Thomas Pelham Clinton, 3rd Duke of Newcastle, caught whooping cough. On the 18th May he died when a blood vessel ruptured, the result of vomiting induced by the cure prescribed for his ailment. He was in his 43rd year and had been Duke for a mere fifteen months since the death of his father on 22nd February 1794. He died without realizing the nature and extent of his inheritance.

Thomas's eldest son Henry Pelham Fiennes Pelham Clinton, born on 30th January 1785 and still too young for Eton, succeeded to the title and estates. As was standard practice then he became a ward of court and the Newcastle Estates were held in Chancery. The 4th Duke entered Eton in 1796 and left at the age of eighteen in 1801. Instead of moving on to Oxford or Cambridge the young Duke, assuming the Treaty of Amiens had ended the Napoleonic War, was taken by his mother on a family tour of France in 1802. The Peace of Amiens was short-lived, however, and on the recommencement of hostilities the Duke, with a number of other English people, was interned in France.

His enforced stay lasted four years during which time he "celebrated" coming of age on 30 January 1806. Whilst enduring this period of comparative inactivity the Duke observed and encountered at first hand the egalitarianism of France after the revolution. According to accounts the experience "...did nothing to expand his mind and everything to inspire him with a fear and hatred of liberal institutions". He missed the mellowing effect of a father's wisdom. On his return, aged 22 years, he was considered too old to go to Oxford and he was now a member of the Upper House of Parliament. The Duke became a diehard Conservative who violently opposed Parliamentary reform, Catholic emancipation and Protestant dissent He was at times arrogantly proud to be considered by many the most hated man in England. He feared no one, and indeed in 1839 after he had refused to withdraw an offensive letter to the Lord Chancellor, the Queen dispensed with his services as Lord Lieutenant of Nottinghamshire. Since his Nottingham estates included several large plots in the town as well as the Castle and Yard, Standard Hill, the King's Meadows and Nottingham Park, the effects of the quirks of the Fourth Duke on the town were substantial.

In the late eighteenth and early nineteenth centuries Nottingham was ruled by a Whig oligarchy consisting mainly of non-conformists, with a reputation for fighting for civil and religious freedom. Friction with the Duke was unavoidable. This was to be the struggle which emphatically influenced the way the old Castle Park was transformed during the nineteenth century into the prestigious residential area of The Park Estate.

Nottingham Park lies in a natural horseshoe; from Derby Road to the north it descends and opens to Castle Boulevard a good half mile and 250 feet lower to the south. The centre of Nottingham is close to the east, while to the west and north-west are the parishes of Lenton and Radford. The Park's width varies and in places is rather more than half a mile.

In the eighteenth century Nottingham was an attractive town whose charms were much admired by visitors. Its population in 1779 was 17,584. Once the movement from the country to the towns had started, those seeking employment increased the population to 28,801 by the time of the first national census in 1801. By 1821 it had leapt to 40,190 and ten years later it had reached 50,220.

These newcomers needed accommodation. So limited was the available land, confined within the bounds of the old town because of the Burgesses' hold over the outlying common lands, that the once famed gardens and other open spaces were lost to the demands of housing. In many cases this new housing, rapidly erected, was of a very poor quality.

Nottingham Park, so near at hand and yet so much like open country, became a great attraction. With the 'Castle' or Ducal Palace no longer a great house and with its owner absent, strolling across the Park became quite a custom with the local inhabitants. The Park was the lung of the overcrowded town, but what these occasional promenaders failed to recognise was that this was private property. The 'blind eyes' turned by the Duke's local agents went unappreciated. So when rumours of the possible development of the Park were first heard there were loud protests in the town at this outrageous act.

Reflecting the vicissitudes of the Newcastle family, there were several attempts to develop the Park from 1780, when the Second Duke gave an acre of the old Castle's Northern Bailey for the building of the General Hospital, to the final flurry of Edwardian villas on Huntingdon Drive a century and a quarter later. During this time particularly from 1854, the old deer park was transformed into a masterpiece of Victorian enterprise. It became an estate of splendid houses, providing homes for many of the town's business and municipal elite, close to the town and yet naturally shut off from it.

2. The Castle's Park

The Park was originally part of the domain of the King's Castle at Nottingham. Nottingham's Castle dates from 1068 when William the Conqueror ordered a motte and bailey structure to be built on the edge of the Bunter Sandstone outcrop 130 feet above the River Leen. This impregnable site lay to the west of the Saxon settlement located on the small sandstone plateau around St. Mary's Church. The constructor and first keeper of the Castle was William Peverel. Highly regarded by the Conqueror, he was further rewarded with the great fief, the Honour of Nottingham. During the reign of Henry II (1133-89) a later William Peverel had licence to enclose ten "forest" acres of land to form an "orchard". This would be some 500 statute acres, and as the Park in later surveys varied between 130 and 140 statute acres, much of the original enclosure must have been surrendered after the 12th century.

As a fringe area of Sherwood Forest the Park would be well stocked with game, and deer would roam in and out of the area.

Nottingham Castle became a favourite Royal residence, and successive Kings improved it. For over four centuries, until Henry Tudor defeated Richard III at Bosworth in 1485, it was the principal Royal castle in the Midlands. The King and his court would often stay for a week or more, an occasion when Parliaments were sometimes held. The Royal Park would conveniently provide those gatherings with food and sport, hunting and jousting.

The River Leen formed the southern boundary of the Park and defined the Castle's grazing land, the King's Meadow, the water meadows between the Rivers Leen and Trent. The Normans diverted the Leen to flow under the Castle rock where it powered the Castle mill and serviced the great ponds there, which were constructed to supply the Castle with fresh fish.

In the 14th century a small portion within the Park was enclosed to form a food store to supply the armies of Edward II in wars against the Scots. It is possible there were more formal pleasure gardens; the Queen's Garden was laid out for Queen Isabella some time before the Mortimer intrigue of 1330, and is presumed to have been near the present tennis courts.

The only intrusion in the Park was the Chapel of St. Mary de la Roche adjoining the Leen. This "chapel", probably a hermitage based on a cave system hewn out of a low sandstone cliff, had close links with Lenton Priory. Later deserted and thereby losing their religious purpose, the caves had a variety of uses. They were for a time, perhaps not without reason, known as the "Papist Holes". Much later in the nineteenth century, they were displayed as the "Druid Holes" and used as refreshment rooms by the nearby Bowling Club.

The Castle became increasingly dilapidated during the Tudor period. James I no longer required it as a residence and granted the ruins and its park to the Earl of Rutland in 1623. The Earl appears to have seen the Castle as a source of building materials, for he removed "tymbre, lede and tyle". Thus it is hardly surprising that Charles I visiting the town in 1634 chose to stay at Thurland Hall, the residence of the Earl of Clare, the Castle being considered unsuitable! During the Civil War the Castle was commandeered, patched-up and held for Parliament by Colonel John Hutchinson. His wife Lucy describes the Park at this time in her *Memoirs* of her husband: *Behind it (the Castle) was a place called the Park, that belonged to the Castle but then had neither deer nor trees in it, except one tree growing under the castle which was almost a prodigy for from the root to the top there was not a straight twig or branch on it, some said it was planted by King Richard the Third and resembled him that set it.*

The first map showing the bounds of the Park is the southern portion of a huge manuscript map prepared to accompany a Survey of the Forest of Sherwood taken in 1609. Recorded are "One lodge and a park called Nottingham Park next to the town adjoining whereof part of it is in Lenton Lordship in the occupation of the King freeholder containing 129 acres 3 roods 9 perches". Nine closes of meadow including the "King's Meadowe in all 108 acres 0 roods 32 perches in the occupation of William Bradwell, with the King freeholder" are also listed. A rather crude *Mappe of the Lordshippe of Lenton and Radford* dated 10th May 1632 and compiled by Richard Smythe does show the western boundary of the Park looking very much like that on the more exact nineteenth century maps.

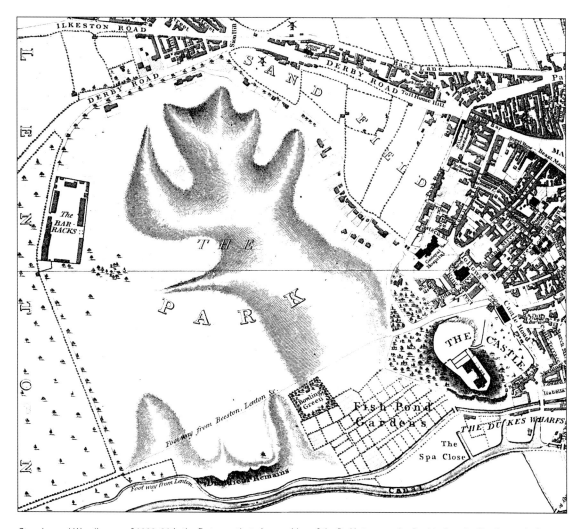

Staveley and Wood's map of 1829-30 is the first map that gives an idea of the Park's topography. By this time the first houses by Peter Frederick Robinson have been erected on the periphery of the Park.

3. The First Dukes of Newcastle

In May 1651 Hutchinson, fearful of the power of Cromwell's military dictatorship, obtained permission of the Parliamentary Council of State to demolish the Castle. The authorized destruction ". . . was speedily executed . . ." Nevertheless when Cromwell ". . . saw the Castle pulled down, he was heartily vexed at it". Much of the building material was sold off or used for repair work around the town.

In 1662, shortly after the restoration of the monarchy, William Cavendish, Earl of Newcastle, former tutor to Charles II and a staunch Royalist, purchased the ruins and the Park from George Villiers, 2nd Duke of Buckingham. Cavendish, created 1st Duke of Newcastle in 1665, cleared what remained of the Medieval Castle and in 1674 started to build his Italianate Renaissance palace. It was completed, after his death in 1679, at a cost of £14,000.

As the building work proceeded, so the Park was re-enclosed and restocked with deer. A survey of the Castle and Park undertaken in 1663 and perhaps related to its purchase, gave its area as a little over 131 acres with the distance round the Park as "1 mile and three quarters and the fourth of a quarter". It is recorded that the herd of deer was sold off in 1717 but stags brought in by cart were hunted in the Park as late as 1798. Poaching was a problem as was the reluctance of the expert deer stalkers of the town to share their haul with the estate keepers. Meanwhile, townsfolk were allowed to graze cattle for a fee.

The Newcastles failed to produce male heirs and the modern line commenced in 1714 when a nephew of the original stock, Thomas Pelham (Holles) was re-created 1st Duke of Newcastle. He died in 1768, and again there were no heirs, his nephew Henry Pelham Clinton becoming the 2nd Duke. Since then there has been direct descent. The 1st Duke was the great Whig politician who was twice Prime Minister between 1754-56, and 1757-62.

According to Hicklin (1836), quoting a note made by the artist Paul Sandby on his drawing of the Castle (1776), the late Duke had laid out a plan for the finest garden in this part of England, to cover not less than 60 acres, adjoining the Castle. The plan was subsequently abandoned. The 2nd Duke cared little for the Castle, for the social whirl was now centred on London. The last great ball was held in 1776 by the Earl of Lincoln to mark his appointment to the Colonelcy of the Nottingham Militia. With the Castle no longer required as a residence the building was let as apartments. By the end of the century one observer noted that an air of desertion pervaded the entire building.

This was the time when the Park was increasingly used as a recreational area, the local inhabitants in effect regarding it as their own. To be fair the elders of the town tried to protect the Park. Contemporary newspapers carried offers of rewards for information leading to the conviction of those guilty of wilful damage in the Park.

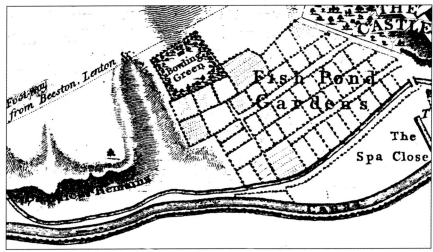

The Fishpond Gardens were established between 1792-4 when soil removed for the foundations of the Barracks was used to fill in the long neglected Castle fishpond. This map extract of 1830 shows the old Park Bowling Green, established c. 1807 and the valley later to become Park Ravine. In the 1840s another bowling green, the Wellington, later called the Newcastle was laid out above the "Remains".

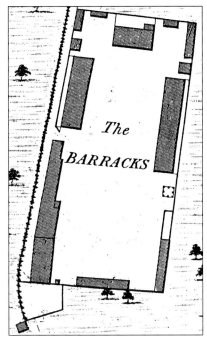

The Cavalry Barracks were built on a plot of about four acres in the north-west of the Park during 1792-3 by S. Stretton and Son. Additions of 1797-8-9 brought the total cost of the Barracks close to £20,000. (Ref: Stretton MSS).

The first commercial encroachment on the Park and Castle grounds occurred c. 1720 when the old Castle fishpond (Reed Pond of 1663) was leased to the Waterworks Company for use as a reservoir. Alas, the Company failed to maintain the reservoir and it became a swamp, often a haunt of fishermen or wild fowlers. In 1792 it was largely filled in with soil brought from the foundations of the Cavalry Barracks then under construction for the Government in the North West corner of the Park. Within two years the Fishpond Gardens were ready for cultivation and plots here and in the Castle grounds were available for renting. These gardens with their rich fertile soil were much sought after by the townsmen, who often erected a small summer house on their portion. The quality and abundance of the vegetables, fruit and flowers grown gained quite a reputation locally.

In 1792 the 7th Light Dragoons were billeted in the town and it was appropriate that on the 21st August the first stone of the new Barracks was laid by their commanding officer. The site of four acres was leased from the Duke of Newcastle for 60 years at £80 per annum. The buildings were completed within a year by S. and W. Stretton; the total cost including extensions of 1797-8-9 was almost £20,000. For 60 years some of the most famous regiments of the British Army were stationed there and their parades and ceremonies became a feature of town life. Local Magistrates called on them in times of civil disturbance to help restore order.

A small Riding School for the Nottingham Troop of the Yeomanry Cavalry was built in 1798 just below the Castle Lodge by William Stretton. Vacated by the Cavalry, the building was enlarged and used as a drill hall by the Robin Hood Rifles from 1872. Later it was used for a variety of purposes until it was demolished in 1926.

4. The Nottingham Estate

The 3rd Duchess of Newcastle was 35 when her husband died. Still a young woman, within five years she had remarried. (on the 7th February 1800 she married Colonel, later Lieutenant General, Sir Charles Gregor Cranford of Ranby Hall, Retford). However in 1795, now the Dowager Duchess, she was bewildered. She had no real idea of the size, importance and value of the Newcastle Estates. The Duke being a minor, trustees were appointed through whom she had to run the estate; these lawyers in turn were advised by a number of local agents.

On Badder and Peet's map of 1744 there is no direct access to the Park from Friar Lane or Hounds Gate. The Outer Bailey Wall here is intact.

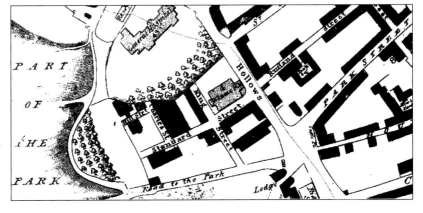

Wild and Smith's map of 1820 shows not only "Road to the Park" cut in 1809 but also a pathway along the line of the later Park Valley leading to the Park Steps.

Correspondence received by the Duchess in 1799 suggests that with remarriage in the offing she had decided that Nottingham Castle in particular, the Park with Standard Hill, and other property in the town were increasingly difficult to manage. To get some idea of their potential she consulted a number of local agents. One drawback however was whether land and property or money would in the long term be of greater benefit for the young Duke. This tricky question was made more difficult because although the Dowager Duchess was one of the trustees of the estates, the running of the states was in the hands of a receiver, appointed by Chancery, who reported periodically to Chancery.

The Duchess consulted one of the other trustees, a London solicitor Gilbert Jones, for clarity on disposal. His reply dated 30th December 1799 informed the Duchess:

My Lady Duchess,
The Court of Chancery ordinarily directs the sale of property belonging to Infants to be by publick Auction before one of the Masters; but if a purchaser could be found who would buy the Castle at Nottingham by private contract such a Contract might be entered into subject to the approbation of the Court ... whether it would be for the Interest of the Duke ...
Thus Jones reminded the Duchess that whilst trustees could make recommendations to Chancery, the trustees would need the support of Chancery for any disposal.

Much of the correspondence with agents is of the same date. The Castle was a liability. John Deakin writing from Bagthorpe Farm 31st December 1799 suggests "If Nottingham Castle should not be sold ... let it upon short leases in several divisions (4 or 5) which would increase the rent and save the expense at present attending it, and retain it in the family". The disposal of the Park worried him: "With respect to Nottingham Park I beg leave to state that if it was now offered to be sold it would greatly injure the sale of the Building land and Houses in Nottingham ... Besides I think the Park nearly the very last property in point of real interest the Duke should part with ..."

A little later (3rd February, 1800) Mr. W. Gauntley of Bakewell, an agent of the Duke of Rutland, outlined action prior to any comprehensive development of the Park: contour maps, sections, water supplies, layout of roads etc. "The setting out (of) the Park into lots is a very important Business and will require much information and the most serious attention". He ends encouragingly "I expect purchasers would come from distant places for lots in the Park". Other letters stress the need for secrecy". . . . it will be prudent also not to mention the sale of any part of the Castle or Park Hill (until) all the other be disposed of . . ."

Perhaps the most important letter is again from John Deakin. Dated 7th May 1802 it accompanies plans of the Castle and Grounds and of Standard Hill. Deakin proposes a strategy for disposal: "and respecting the sale of Standard Hill I would advise that part to be disposed of first, in rather small lots, as offering the whole at once might materially injure the value of both that and the Castle part of the estate and until Standard Hill is sold I would wish it not to be made known that the Castle and Yard may afterwards be disposed of. I will get a valuation of the materials of Nottingham Castle by Taylor and Stretton as soon as possible." How significant is the word "materials"?

The sale of the land on Standard Hill was arranged. In fact the sale is set down in the Stretton Manuscripts as 23rd August 1802: "The piece of land called the Standard Hill (containing 9080 square yards) sold at 12/- a yard by the Duke of Newcastle." However, the Duke's enforced stay in France and other events put off the sale until early in 1807. Then a revised layout of Standard Hill, now with 32 lots fetched nearly £7,000.

On his return from France, the Duke now 21 was now master of his inheritance. In his own right a wealthy man, he added to his wealth when not long after his return to England he married Georgina Elizabeth Mundy of Shipley, Derbys; heiress to an estate of £190,000. The marriage took place at Lambeth Palace on 18th July 1807, and was solemnized by the Archbishop of Canterbury.

From the outset Standard Hill was to be a superior development, and to ensure this all purchasers agreed through a covenant . . . to pave and keep in repair one half of the streets so far as they respectively extend in front, or by the side of his lot; to make foot pavements four feet broad; and not to build any houses upon the premises, of less value than £25 per annum nor erect any manufactory or suffer any obnoxious trade whatever to be carried on. There were four imposing streets, Hill Street, Charles Street, Standard Street and King Charles Street, Four lots bordering on The Hollows (St. James's Terrace) were reserved for a new church, St. James's. A private Act of Parliament was needed before this church could be erected and there was much opposition to it before the Bill received the Royal Assent. St. James's was designed by William Stretton and paid for by public subscriptions amounting to almost £13,000. It was completed in 1808. Stretton was one of the signatories of the Standard Hill lease and he built three of the first houses there 1810-14 at a cost of c. £4,000. St. James's Church was demolished in 1936 and a Nurses' Hostel, since demolished, was erected on the site. Other buildings, part of the expansion of the General Hospital, have destroyed most of the old street pattern of Standard Hill, and only a part of King Charles's Street survives.

Standard Hill was extra-parochial, that is belonging to no parish and therefore paying no poor rate; its status caused a great deal of discontent. Several attempts were made to change this and the town tested the extent of its jurisdiction over Standard Hill. An Act of Parliament finally resolved the problem; Justices of the Peace, empowered to determine and fix boundaries between counties and other places for rating purposes, "...fixed the boundary of the County so as to include the whole of Standard Hill."

Mainly through the enterprise of officers stationed at the Barracks, the old Park Bowling Green was laid out and opened c.1807. This plot on the western edge of the Fishpond Gardens close to the footpath to Lenton and Beeston was rented from the Newcastle Estate for £12 per annum.

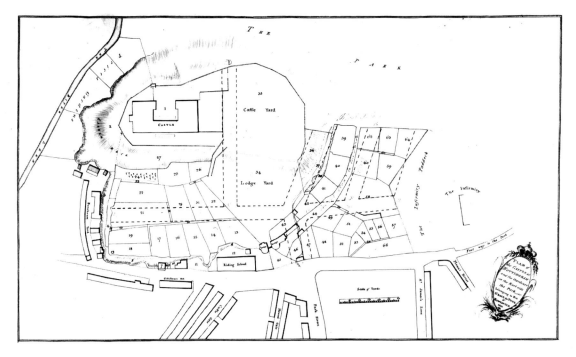

Brown's plan of the Castle and gardens marking out the proposed new street layout (Dashed lines) 1801 (N.U.M.D. Ne P 2)

In 1809 the Park Passage, an improved access road to the Park, was constructed by filling in the Castle moat near the lodge (Gatehouse) up to a depth of 20 feet. The Park's aspect was improved by the planting of larch, spruce, elm and oak trees. Grazing was allowed and the agistment (grazing fees) brought in over £500 in 1808-9. A cow-catcher was paid a mere 10/6d.; but the mole-killer received £1-11-6d!

In June 1812 a mortgage with a token value of £12,000 was taken out on the Castle and Park, the object being to buy out the interest of the Dowager Duchess for £5 per cent. The area of Castle and Park was reckoned to be 153 acres 3 roods 30 perches.

5. The First Tentative Development

In January 1821 as a way of creating work for the unemployed of the town "the Short Hill in the Park was lowered and the valley below raised." Then early in 1822 the Duke engaged the services of a minor local architect and surveyor John Jephson to start development on the edge of the Park. The *Nottingham Journal*, 11th May 1822, carried the story. *We understand that his Grace the Duke of Newcastle has it in contemplation to allow a portion of the Park, near this town, to be built upon. The plan comprehends the space on the hillside from the entrance at the back of the Infirmary to Sion Hill (now Canning Circus). If the design should be carried out into execution it will form one of the most magnificent crescents in the Kingdom.*

Later in that month on 27th May, the Duke's eldest child Anna Maria died. On that day the 4th Duke started his Diaries; a personal record that continued until 1849. Perhaps above all, as far as Nottingham was concerned, the diary entries show the Duke was more kindly disposed towards the town than the local newspapers and the Town Council would admit. Meanwhile during June, Jephson advertised in the *Journal* plots of land on Nottingham Park Terrace varying in size between 500 to 1,000 square yards at moderate rents on sixty year leases. A document headed *Explanation to the Plan of Nottingham Park & Proposals relative to the same* survives, though the plan is missing. Dated March 22nd 1822, it was probably probably written by Jephson.

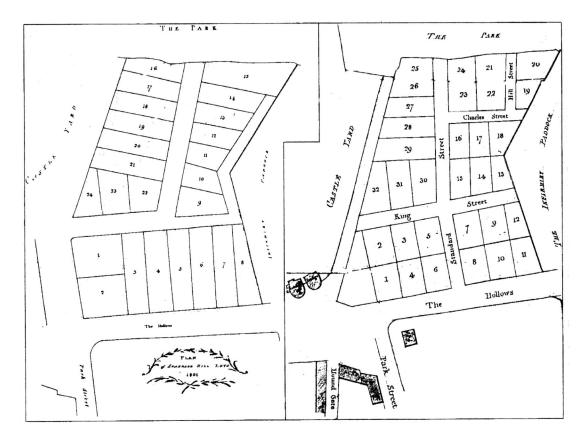

Plans of proposed plots on Standard Hill of 1801 (left) and 1807 (right)
(N.U.M.D. Ne P 3, N.A.O. M 4763).

On the 22nd September the Duke's wife Georgiana died two days after giving birth to twins; one a girl was still-born, and the other, hastily christened George, died on 7th October. Without doubt the Duke's grief, his family life shattered, the extra parental responsibility of coping with his ten surviving children taking precedent; together with the financial complexities of settlement all contributed to the postponement of the Park's development. Jephson was paid £23-15-6d. for "Surveying the Park and making plans and elevations of intended houses." Alas, again, this work is lost.

No doubt hoping for a rewarding career in the Duke's service Jephson split from the building and surveying partnership he had with the better known architect William Surplice late in 1822. It is likely that Jephson's ideas were eventually felt to be unworthy of "... one of the finest building sites in the United Kingdom." He certainly plummets into architectural obscurity, however he did produce drawings of the Duke's Thurland Hall in 1825. Although development of the Park was on hold, there were those in the town who were well aware of its development potential. On the 23rd September 1824 a proposal was made to the Duke to let the Park on a lease of 99 years. The Duke noted "I shall require better terms and shall give a shorter lease, if I accept the plan at all." The following day he wrote to the architect (Sir) Robert Smirke "to enquire if he can put me in a way of so disposing of the land in Nottingham Park on lease as at once to be profitable and be highly ornamental to the Town." Smirke was already working for the Duke, preparing plans for a memorial church for his late wife at West Markham in North Nottinghamshire.

This particular diary entry closes with the Duke well disposed towards the town. "I should wish to infuse a new spirit into the people of Nottingham and give them a taste for the fine arts - a beautiful thing might be made of the Park if properly planned and executed."

Two months later, on 23rd November, the Duke was visited by William Surplice who wished to lease the Park for building purposes. The Duke appears willing to negotiate the terms and insists "the plan to be ornamental, the houses good & the whole a credit to the good taste of the capital of the County." As noted, by coincidence or otherwise, Surplice had been in partnership with the unfortunate Jephson. At this time the original unknown speculator on the Park's development is revealed as Charles Wright, the son of the Nottingham banker, Ichabod Wright of Mapperley Hall. The Duke's dealings with Wright continued into January 1825, Wright being most persistent and the Duke most suspicious, but in the end Wright's various propositions about leasing were dismissed - at one point the Duke commented "he wishes to obtain of possession of Nottingham Park & then destroy it as a good thing & merely turn it to his own grovelling advantage."

The Duke invited his agents Mr Chambers and Mr Leeson to Clumber on 21st December 1824 "to talk over & settle matters preparatory to making final arrangements about Nottm Park." This seems to imply that the Duke had rekindled his interest and optimism about developing the Park, most likely without involving Charles Wright and his stream of confusing offers on leaseholds and terms.

William Surplice meanwhile had switched his interest to the Duke's Thurland Hall paddock and on 28th March 1825 an agreement was signed giving Surplice 20 lots on a lease of 65 years at a rent of £56.

On 2nd April 1825, possibly introduced by Robert Smirke, the Duke met with the architect Mr Hakewill. He "settled with him to go to Nottingham for the purpose of planning the new town in the Park in the best and most advantageous manner."

Hakewill did carry out surveys of the Park during 1825, but soon he is replaced as the favoured architect by Peter Frederick Robinson. At one time an assistant to Henry Holland, Robinson (1776-1858), built very little, but his books of 'Designs' were very influential. As an architect he has been described by the eminent architectural writer Sir John Summerson as a 'style conjuror.' The Duke's first meeting with Robinson took place in Nottingham on 30th November 1825. With the assistance of a local steward they made a thorough survey of the Park the following day and eventually drew up a development plan. The Duke recorded his hope that "the scheme will take well & that it will be highly beneficial & productive to me & eminently ornamental & beneficial to the Town & County".

Robinson was at this time (1823-6) working in Leamington Spa preparing a 'Plan for the buildings about to be erected on the Estate of Edward Willes', the streets around the later Beauchamp Square. There is some similarity in the layout with his later 'Plan of Nottingham Park the Property of His Grace the Duke of Newcastle, Showing the intended Lines of Building', dated May 1827.

With Robinson proceeding with the plans, the Duke appears to have received assurances from un-named sources that the development was sure to be successful. On 16th October 1826 the Duke contacted Robinson about an immediate commencement of building in the Park. On 20th-21st November the Duke came to Nottingham to arrange with the architect the final preparations for building. "In the Spring we shall commence building the first house of a range ... no delay shall take place when the proper season for building arrives."

A diary entry for 28th November 1826 records "My plans at Nottingham have been announced & I have recd offers to build some houses." These plans, Robinson's plan of May 1827, have a rectangular layout influenced by the London squares of John Nash, which completely ignores the topography of the Park.

Top: Houses from that "style conjuror" Peter Frederick Robinson erected in the late 1820s and 1830s can be seen on the rim of the Park. Park Terrace left, right (rear view) and bottom right; Park Valley bottom left

Lower: This engraving by T. Picken 1840 depicts the Park as a flat featureless area following on from Robinson's plan of 1827. A church and a tunnel entrance in the railway style of the day have been added. Early houses are drawn in, centre top, as is the church of St. James, Standard Hill, close to the Castle. (L.S.L.)

Above: The promenaders can be seen in this rural idyll Nottingham Park 1837 by Thomas Allom. The houses on the Ropewalk and Park Terrace are shown, whilst down below the first houses on a Park Valley track can be picked out. (L.S.L.)

Gregory (G) and Newcastle (N) Estates boundary marker

In this portion of "Nottingham from the Meadows" by Henry Burn 1846 the train from Derby is seen passing below the park and the Castle on its way to Nottingham station. When the service was inaugurated on 30th May 1839 thousands on the lower part of the Park cheered the train on its journey to Derby. (45 minutes stopping, 25 minutes non-stop). (L.S.L.)

Below: The Park Steps were probably cut into an existing sloping track in the late 1820s when access to the first houses in what became Park Valley was needed. They have been continually upgraded since the early 1830s.

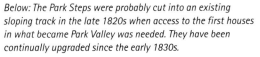

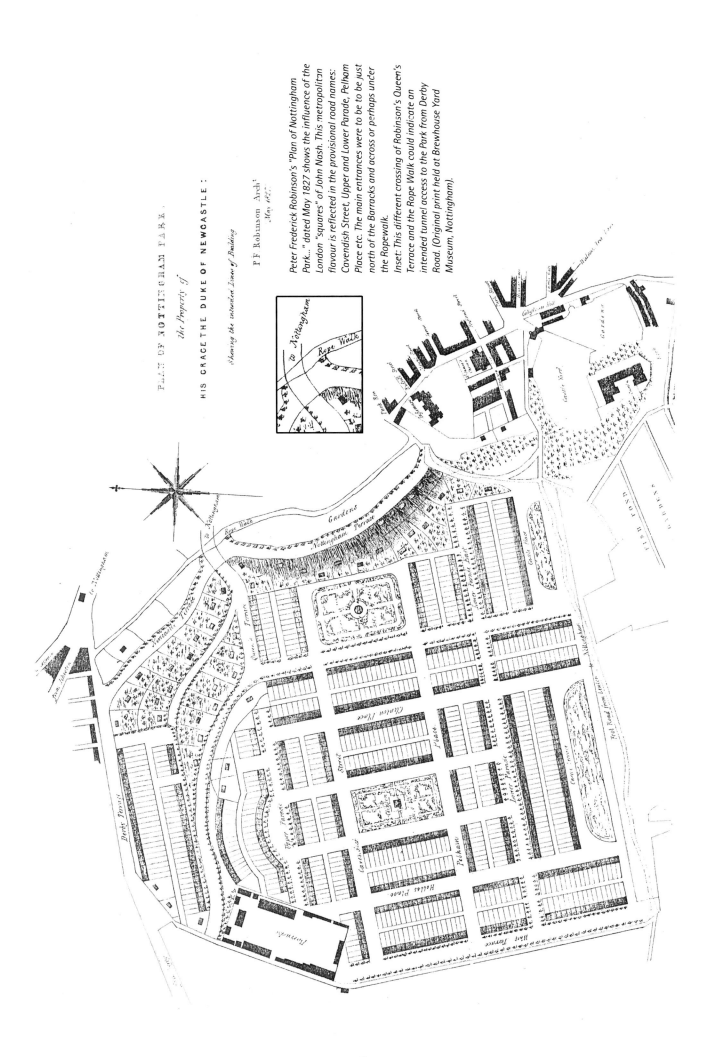

PLAN OF NOTTINGHAM PARK,
the Property of
HIS GRACE THE DUKE OF NEWCASTLE:
Shewing the intended Lines of Building

P F Robinson Arch.t
May 1827

Peter Frederick Robinson's "Plan of Nottingham Park..." dated May 1827 shows the influence of the London "squares" of John Nash. This metropolitan flavour is reflected in the provisional road names: Cavendish Street, Upper and Lower Parade, Pelham Place etc. The main entrances were to be to be just north of the Barracks and across or perhaps under the Ropewalk.
Inset: This different crossing of Robinson's Queen's Terrace and the Rope Walk could indicate an intended tunnel access to the Park from Derby Road. (Original print held at Brewhouse Yard Museum, Nottingham).

No doubt local people realized what was about to happen before the *Nottingham Journal* leaked the story on 7th April 1827: *The long projected plan of setting out the Park near this town in lots, and letting the same on building leases, is about to be carried into effect and already the ground has been partly marked out...but space will still be left for a promenade although much of its original beauty will naturally be destroyed. The inhabitants generally, will regret this, as a curtailment of an enjoyment peculiarly delightful to them, and which has existed from time immemorial.* A week later, Friday 13th April, the *Nottingham Review* carried the news: *Last Saturday to the great regret of many observers a commencement was made of the intended alterations in the Park by beginning to dig out the foundations of a house (Mr. Boothby's) at the outside of the hill near to Bachelor's Walk ..*

On 21st June 1827, the Duke signed the first agreement for building leases in the Park to William Patterson. Patterson was the builder who several years later with the young architect Thomas Chambers Hine formed the partnership of Patterson and Hine. Robinson informs the Duke he is convinced that "the scheme will now gradually proceed towards accomplishment, as so many enquiries are making & several offers made."

Robinson reported again to the Duke on 1st September 1827 on how well building was progressing "already several houses are erecting, three are built." Two days later the Duke and his son, Lord Lincoln, met with Robinson, who conducted them around the building projects. The appropriate diary entry ends "...(there are) many offers for fresh buildings of the best description."

Well-spaced diary entries for 1828 and 1829 refer to the progress made in developing the Park as an estate. On 20th January 1829 with "a great many buildings erected & roads formed" the Duke is moved to add "...the scheme is now a favourite with the Town - so that its success is no longer in doubt." Later that year, on 23rd October, amidst the euphoria the Duke admits "...they are not everything that I could wish" but quickly resumes with "...altogether it is a very great improvement not only to my property but to the Park." Thereafter the Duke appears to have left Robinson to get on with the building work.

There is in the Nottinghamshire Archive Office a copy of the deeds of **8-10 Park Valley** made out to William Melville of Standard Hill. The deeds are dated 31st December 1828; they are signed by P. Robinson, of Lower Brook Street, London, and unexpectedly have an elevation drawing of the houses.

So development had started; minor initial delays fired hopeful rumours that work had ceased. However other buildings on the Ropewalk and the first houses on Park Terrace soon followed. On Staveley and Wood's Maps of 1830-1 **these early houses on Park Terrace, the rural nos. 13 and 14, and the Regency pairs 7-8, 9-10 and 11-12** are shown as well as a number on the Ropewalk, several of which have long been demolished. The Park Terrace houses are almost certainly by Robinson and most likely built by William Patterson. It is said that as the residents of the Ropewalk saw the Park Terrace houses rising and cutting off their uninterrupted views to the south of the county they attacked the surprised builders who were rescued by the constables!

Derby Terrace alongside the present northern gates was started about this time. It is particularly interesting for it is considered to be the prototype of the housing Robinson had planned for the Park. (On his plan he had 26 houses with gardens in Derby Terrace).

The Park Passage was greatly enlarged in 1829, as were the Park Steps; the Ropewalk was improved in 1830 and early in 1831 North Road was established, a deviation from the 1827 plan. This work and other routine and development-related activities were supervised by Thomas Winter, the Duke's agent; in the period 1827-32 well over £3,000 was invested in the Park.

What was progressing as a routine development was shattered by the firing of the Castle on 10th October 1831. Besides the local antagonism directed against the 4th Duke because of the impending loss of the Park's recreational facilities, he was also the object of increasing national animosity. For over twenty years many people had censured his extreme Tory line, and they were now aggravated by his hostility to the Great Reform Bill. He voted against its 3rd reading. When on the evening of 8th October 1831, news reached Nottingham that the House of Lords had thrown out the second Reform Bill, a sequence of events started which led eventually to the storming of the empty Castle and its virtual destruction by fire. Although at the time his Nottingham Castle was not occupied and in a semi-ruinous state, it represented Newcastle and therefore was a prime target.

(Whilst it is generally accepted that Nottingham Castle was in a ruinous state at this time, two entries in the Duke's diaries indicated that some attempt to repair the Castle had taken place. On 1st April 1824 the Duke notes "on inspecting the Castle I found it in bad repair... all in a very dilapidated state". Then the entry for 23rd August 1824 records "In Nottingham, walked to the Castle where I am thoroughly repairing the whole & projected some improvements to the canal side.")

The Duke first heard of the fire in a conversation with Lord Melbourne after attending a debate in the House of Lords on 11th October. Melbourne reported he had had bad news from Nottingham. In his diary the Duke recorded that Melbourne had said "...that Nottingham was in a shocking state & that the rioters had set fire to Nottm Castle." He own reaction was "I have heard nothing about it, & I hope it is not true, but I much fear that it is..."

It was some time before the Duke ventured to Nottingham; when he did on 16th November 1832 "...the fog was so thick I could not see the Castle. I felt heart sick at being in the neighbourhood of so much villainy, spoliation & malicious mischief."

The Reform Bill was passed without much trouble in the early summer of 1832 while the Duke was pursuing compensation at the Leicester Assizes for the gutting of his Castle. The Duke maintained that by the passing of the Bill he had lost the patronage and interest in six boroughs, a loss he assessed at £200,000. This merely confirmed what many felt, "...his appetite for jobbery was insatiable."

Whilst the Duke claimed £31,000 compensation, much of the hearing was spent determining who would pay. Eventually the Hundred of Broxtowe was deemed liable. As expert witnesses the Duke called P. F. Robinson and Edward Staveley, the Borough Surveyor. The Hundred of Broxtowe relied on Henry Moses Wood (Staveley's assistant), William Cubitt the London building contractor and James Nicholson, an architect and builder of Southwell. They agreed that the rebuilding of the Castle would cost £15,400 but to be made as good as new the cost would rise to £21,000, the amount awarded to the Duke. Hidden in the transcript of the case are interesting facts about the Park at that time. Wood related: "Part of the Park is set apart for building ground, there are now from forty to sixty houses in the Park." Robinson stated "There are many houses in the Park on the Terrace which continues from Standard Hill round till it comes to Derby Road. I attempted to make them look well. The building of the houses on Derby Road would be rather an improvement than a detriment to the Park." To end his evidence Robinson admitted "I cannot say how many acres there are in the Park."

Did the attack on his Castle influence the Duke's plans for the Park? Work in hand was completed. William Dearden's Map of Nottingham 1834 shows the **Regency houses on Park Terrace Nos. 5-6, 3-4, 1-2** as well as Robinson's distinctive nos. **15-17, the "Italian Villas" and a "lodge" at the North Gate.** No new work was started for some time. Perhaps the Park's natural features were rescued from Robinson through the civil unrest, for his designs demanded a levelled site. It is possible that had the Duke received his full compensation he would have pulled down the Castle's shell and erected several villas from Robinson's copious imagination. Both seemed to have favoured quantity at that time.

In the town the Duke's derelict Thurland Hall had been demolished, and now the site and other land were sold. The Duke took his money elsewhere. He bought the Hafod Estate near Aberystwyth for £62,000 in April 1835. Four years later he purchased Worksop Manor, close to his own Clumber Estate, for £375,000 from the Duke of Norfolk. These transactions certainly drained the Newcastle finances which were now seldom other than slender.

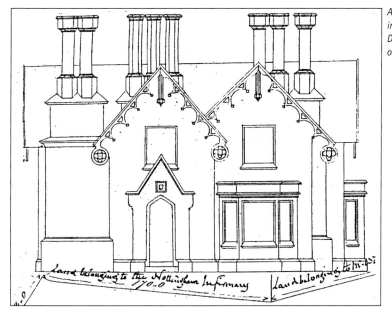

An elevation drawing of 8-10 Park Valley in the deeds of the house, dated 31st December 1828 and signed by P. Robinson of Lower Brook Street, London. (N.A.O.)

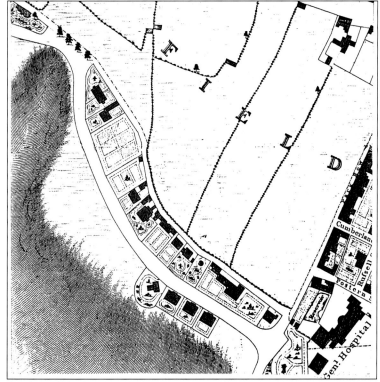

On Staveley and Wood's map of 1830 No,13, 12-11, 10-9, 8-7 Park Terrace are shown together with a number of buildings on the Ropewalk, including No22. By 1834when the earlier of William Dearden's maps was published No. 6-5, 4-3, 2-1 and 15-17 Park Terrace, had been erected to the designs of P. F. Robinson. No. 15-17 are the distinctive Italian Villas. Ten years on, Dearden's later map shows the layout of the roads and the first buildings on the newly enclosed Sandfield (Park Ward). The first houses in the bowl of the Park No. 13, 15 and 17-19 are clearly marked.

Staveley and Wood 1830

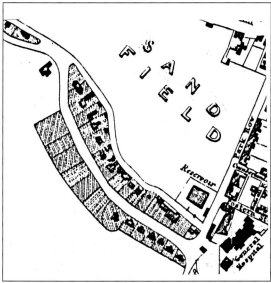

Dearden 1834

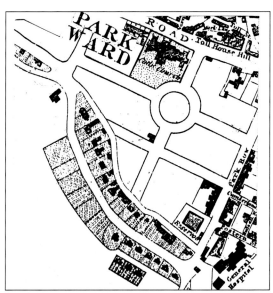

Dearden 1844

An even greater length of time was to pass before the Duke actually saw the ruined Castle. In the diary entry for 8th April 1842 the Duke writes (in Nottingham) "I took my daughters to see the Castle & Park, it was the first time that they had seen them & they were much struck & pleased with the Magnificence of the Situation, & indignant of destruction of Such a noble building - it was the first time that I had Seen it, since it burned."

6. Further Developments: An Access Tunnel Commenced

It is just possible that Robinson first put forward the idea of an access tunnel from the Lower Derby Road, through the sandstone of Park Hill into the valley of the Park. His 1827 plan has some supporting evidence in the form of a strange junction between his Queen's Terrace (Tunnel Road) and his Nottingham Terrace (Park Terrace). As early as 1820 a minor boundary dispute between the Duke's steward and the Town Council ended with the Deputation investigating the matter recommending the Corporation to take the necessary Measures for preventing a Carriage Road being made from Mount Street or Park Row to the Park - the Deputation being of Opinion that "the Duke has not any right to such Road." So a tunnel could solve the problem.

In 1835 the Municipal Reform Act was passed and brought hopes in Nottingham that at last the much needed enclosures could be achieved. The power of the Whig oligarchy was broken by the change in municipal franchise and the objections of the politically impotent Burgesses were removed by negotiated compensation rates for loss of rights. The Duke's local agents and lawyers watched and waited - the release of large amounts of good building land through enclosure was certain to affect land values. Thus the future development of the Park became entangled with the Nottingham enclosure, particularly that near at hand, the Derby Road - Lammas Fields area.

However rather unexpectedly in 1838-9 the first houses in the Park proper appear. These were on Western Terrace and, closer to the intended enclosure, nos. 13, 15 and 17-19 Park Valley, designed by Robinson. Were these houses built to test the market, or with so much investment going elsewhere was that all the estate could finance? Dearden's map of 1844 shows these houses as well as an appreciable increase in the number of Park garden plots. In 1842-3 some 162 plots brought in c. £439 whilst grazing fees raised an extra £330.

The creation of the new gardens on western edge of the Park (Reported in the Nottingham Review 11th March 1842)

STAVELEY & WOOD 1829/30
The row of trees at the western boundary are shown here clearly, if somewhat symbolically. On Dearden's map the changes announced in the newspaper have taken place. The new gardens are shown, also more gardens round the bowling green.

DEARDEN 1844
On both maps:
1 The Barracks 2 Footway from Beeston 3 Bowling Green
4 Footway from Lenton 5 River Leen
6 'Druidical Remains' i.e. the caves

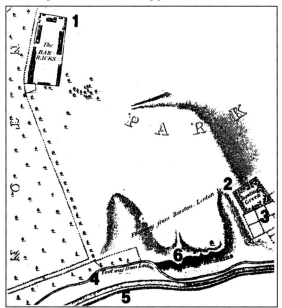
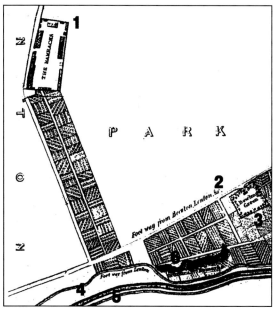

On 1st April 1839 Robert Leason, the Duke's Nottingham solicitor, wrote anxiously to his client: "Another application is making for the inclosure of about 18 acres of open land in the Parish of St. Mary's Nottingham ... between the Derby Turnpike Road and Your Grace's Park. The land is to be laid out for buildings with spacious streets ... It is possible this may have some effect on Your Grace's Estate in the Park but the circumstances of your exceptions from the Burdens of the Town must enhance the value of the Park."

John Buckley, one of the Duke's Nottingham agents, managed to get specially drawn plans of the intended enclosures from the Corporation Surveyor H. M. Wood. He sent them to the Duke with a covering letter on 4th April 1839. He gave a brief account of likely building restrictions and repeated the fears of lower land prices. Most interestingly he says "If a tunnel under the hill to the Park could be effected at the point I have marked with a cross ... it would be far more to Your Grace's advantage." Buckley's cross is roughly below the garden of **15-17 Park Terrace, the 'Italianate Villa'**. On 29 May 1839, a few days before the 1839 Nottingham Derby Road Lammas Fields Enclosure Act was to be presented to Parliament, the Duke received details of the valuation of his Nottingham property from Mr. Buckley. A delighted owner recorded that Buckley "had made amount to an Enormous Sum Somewhere about £180,000 I think for 91 acres in the Park & between 80 & 90 in the Meadows - present rent about £600."

Thus it was important to Newcastle that he protected his interests in the Park against the enclosure of the open fields between the Ropewalk and Derby Road. On 10 June 1839 the Duke went to the House of Lords: "I wish to insert a clause (in the Act) to enable me to make a tunnel for communication - This the parties are unwilling to grant & wished me to be contented with undertaking (?), this I told them I could not be, & upon the attorney for one of the parties saying that he could not advise his clients to consent to a clause - I told him that I should oppose the bill & soon brought him to his senses."

Two days later the Duke's diary entry confirms his successful intervention. "I have endeavoured to secure my interest by introducing a clause into the Bill in Committee tomorrow, which we have drawn & prepared for the purpose - I have been obliged to fight hard to secure this privilege."

The successful outcome of this intervention by the Duke can be seen in part of the text of the 1839 Act:

1839 DERBY ROAD LAMMAS FIELDS INCLOSURE ACT.
2° & 3° VICTORIÆ, *Cap.32 856/857*

That it shall be lawful for the Owner of the said Park for the Time being, and he is hereby authorized and empowered, at any Time or Times hereafter, to make and construct, and from Time to Time to maintain, a Carriage, Horse, and Foot Way, by means of a Tunnel under some Part of the Lands to be inclosed by virtue of this Act, between the said Park called Nottingham Park and the said Turnpike Road or Highway, or between such Park and any One or more of the said Streets to be formed on the Lands to be inclosed by virtue of this Act, such Tunnel to be of such Dimensions as the said Duke, his Heirs or Assigns, shall think proper;

By coincidence on the same day, the 10th June 1839, Thomas Winter submitted to the Duke a "Report on the manner of Constructing a Tunnel and an approach thereto forming an additional entrance into the Nottingham Park"

Winter illustrated his report with a plan of the forthcoming enclosure with two alternative tunnels sketched in - a long tunnel starting on the Derby Road close to the side of the later convent and a shorter tunnel with an entrance in the middle of a new street (College Street) roughly outside the old People's College. Both tunnels had the same exit on the Park side, that proposed by Buckley. Winter had decided "... the more spacious and handsome this road is made, the more valuable the estate becomes therefore the plan no. 1 (the longer) although the most expensive is recommended as the most eligible."

Thomas Winter, the Fourth Duke of Newcastle's Nottingham surveyor, submitted this proposal for a tunnel into the Park to the Duke in June 1839. Notice that he suggested two possible access points. One, for a longer tunnel, would be on Derby Road; the other for a shorter tunnel, on the later College Street. Winter felt the value of the land in the Park would be enhanced by a more prestigious longer tunnel, a point made in the cross section. (N.U.M.D.)

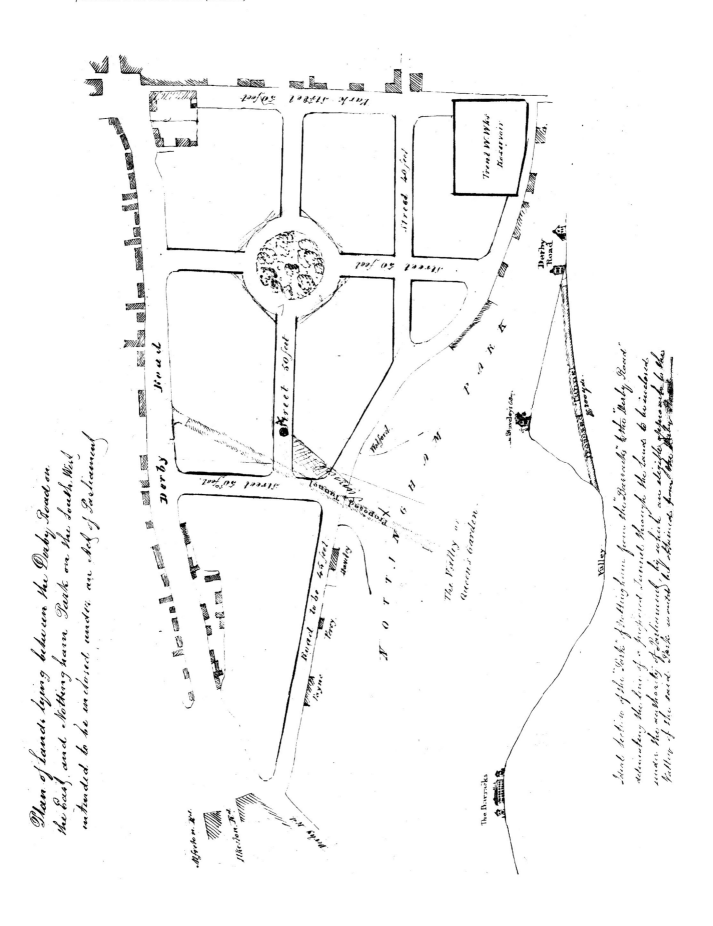

On 1st July 1839 the Derby Road Lammas Fields Inclosure Act received Royal Assent. George Sanderson and John Parkinson, the commissioners appointed, started dividing and allocating the land, in the manner previously agreed, to the registered burgesses. The Duke of Newcastle had no claims to any of this land, but if he could purchase land lying along the line suggested by Winter, Nottingham Corporation could not prevent him tunnelling, with Parliamentary approval, under his own land!

So it was arranged, and a letter from Derby, 29th January 1840 informed the Duke ". . . subject to your Grace's approbation to purchase a thousand yards of land adjoining Nottingham Park to enable your Grace to make a tunnel or other communication with the Park from the roads being formed. . ." Later, on 11th July, 1840, the Duke's receipt was forwarded: "Cash paid Nottingham Inclosure Commissioners Purchase Money of £706-13-0d. Land for Tunnel into the Park." Did the Duke receive special consideration in this matter?

The final award map, published in 1846, has two strips of land quite clearly marked "Duke of Newcastle by Purchase." By now the idea of a Park tunnel was fairly common knowledge. On a coloured engraving by T. Picken "A South West View of Nottingham Park published about 1840, an 'early railway tunnel' entrance is shown in approximately the right position. (A variation of this print appeared in Fyfe's *Rambles Round Nottingham* published in 1856.)

Whilst the Duke was deliberating about a Park tunnel, the townsfolk on 30th May 1839 were very much engaged on observing a momentous event in the history of Nottingham, from the Park. On that day the railway from Nottingham to Derby was opened. As the *Nottingham Review* reported the next day: *Precisely at half past twelve the first engine with carriages attached set off from the station...thousands assembled on the hills in the Park to gaze upon this mighty triumph of mechanical skill...* The undeveloped undulating Park did indeed provide wonderful vantage points.

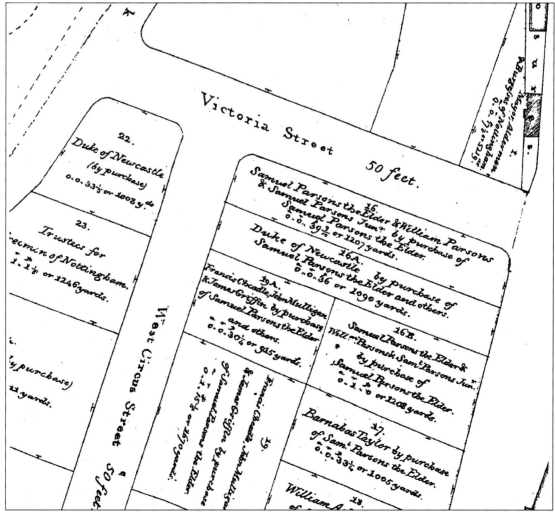

The appropriate portion of the final award map for the Derby Road-Lammas Fields Enclosure (1845) showing the strips of land purchased on behalf of the Duke of Newcastle for the construction of a tunnel into the Park. He now owned the land above the line of the tunnel! Victoria Street is now known as Upper College Street.

With the Duke of Newcastle involved with his purchases of property elsewhere, the Park and its suspended development, with one traced exception, no longer attracted local attention. News of the exception appeared in the *Nottingham Review* of 11th March 1842. Some 70 trees on the western edge of the Park lining the promenade from the Barracks to the footpath to Lenton had been removed and disposed of at auction. They were being replaced by the formation of gardens, the availability of which for letting had already been advertised. The extent of the transformation can be seen by comparing the area involved on Staveley & Wood's map 1829 with that on Dearden's map of 1844.

The *Review's* account was long and flowery: *in a few days the path and trees will be numbered among things that were, It would gladden us exceedingly to witness the conversion of the many fields around Nottingham into gardens, but we think our readers will coincide with us in saying - touch not the Park.* The account ended with an interesting speculation. *Furrows have been cut across the Park as if for the formation of a road, to enter by means of a tunnel, on to the public highway connected with the Derby-road inclosure.*

In fact the Park does not appear again in the Duke's Diaries until 4th November 1843: "I have not looked over the Nottm property for a long while - I have now altered on the spot the several lines of road for communication in & out of the Park, & have devised a general arrangement of the Park property, which I think will be a very great improvement upon the proposed plan." His agent, Thomas Winter, reported that the value of the Park property and land at Basford was "little short of a million of money at £8,000 an acre - or half that sum at about 16s a yard." No wonder the entry concluded "My visit to Nottingham was very satisfactory."

The Duke was in determined mood when he went to Nottingham on 11th April 1844 "in order to make a complete & final arrangement of my property there, so as to turn it to the best advantage. We have been closely... marking out the roads of approach & minutely considering how to form the entrance to the Park from the town combining convenience, economy & beauty." "We mean to try if the rock be sufficiently good and strong to pierce it through & form a natural arch if this can be accomplished it will not only be the handsomest mode, but the saving in expense will be very considerable." He arranged for workmen to test out the qualities of the rock. The entry ends "We have carefully examined the various points of ingress & egress & we have marked out in a rough manner all the lines - but they will require much alteration & further consideration tomorrow."

The next day the Duke made a critical decision: "Having viewed & finally settled all our lines & having proved the rock to be good so that it will be safely excavated, I have settled that a small gallery sufficient to hold two men shall be pierced through the hill at somewhat about the right level from the street in the old Lammas fields to the opposite side in the Park & then a perfect judgement may be formed of its practicability & proper alignment. This & the roads & scenery around with the many peculiarities of gardens, houses, rocks, hills, valleys &c will be as striking & peculiar as anything to be seen anywhere. I am satisfied that there is nothing like it in the Kingdom." Before leaving Nottingham the Duke arranged for surveys to be prepared and submitted to him for approval and execution.

No doubt, after a perusal of these surveys, on 27th May the Duke made a decision about the plan of the new roads in the Park, particularly the approach through the tunnel. On the same day he made arrangements for the sale of his town property in Nottingham: "I have now sold all my house property in Nottingham. The contract for the last house in Pelham St was signed yesterday, & deposit paid" and provisionally for later sales of parts of Basford and the Park.

Almost certainly the locals had heard about and seen what was taking place before the *Nottingham Review* carried the story on 31th May 1844. *NOTTINGHAM PARK: Workmen have been for some time engaged in forming a tunnel through the hill dividing the Park from Derby Road and they are now pretty near half through. This will form a carriage way and will be connected with several new roads to be formed in the Park.* Some members of the Council must have realized the Duke's intentions for quite suddenly at the Council meeting held on 2nd May 1844 the Town Clerk was ordered to enquire into the extent and nature of the Corporation rights over Nottingham Park. No clear answer was given.

Father and Son; Left, the suave fourth Duke of Newcastle from a portrait by H. W. Pickersgill (N.A.O.) Right, the fifth Duke of Newcastle although looking tired and weary was now back as Colonial Secretary, a post he held from 1859 until he resigned in the spring of 1864, several months before his death. (Illustrated London News 22nd December 1860)

In a longer account on 14th June 1844 the *Review* criticised the way the Duke's development of the Park was being used ". . . as a means of supplying his exhausted treasury." Work in progress in the Park was examined and the renewal of the neglected Park Steps was approved. Of the tunnel the article noted *. . . it has been bored considerably more than half way through the hill and the perforation is expected to be complete in about a fortnight.* This proved to be optimistic for the tunnelling stopped and the project was temporarily abandoned. There are two likely reasons for this: enclosure and finance. The General Enclosure Bill was being drafted in 1844 and this related in part to the desirable building land on the Sandfield north of the town, bounded by Mansfield Road, Forest Road and Alfreton Road. It would have been rash to put even extra-parochial land on the market at that time, particularly so with very slender development funds. Financially the Duke's resources were almost gone, principally due to the acquisition of Worksop Manor. Hafod, altered internally and repaired during 1840-1, was put on the market. In March 1844 the *Nottingham Review* reported *The Duke of Newcastle's princely domain of Hafod in Wales is again advertised for sale in the London papers.* Eventually its sale for c. £94,000 was completed on 11th April 1846, no doubt to the relief of the Duke's bankers. In 1848 the Duke sold off part of his enclosure purchase on Derby Road for the erection of a Baptist Chapel. He did retain enough land to ensure an adequate approach to the tunnel between this Derby Road Baptist Chapel and the later Convent.

While attending the Nottingham Assizes on 25th July 1844 the Duke took the opportunity to spend "a very considerable time in the Park - my tunnel is made - I went through it." This of course was the 'two-man gallery' mentioned earlier. He inspected the formation of the new road "at the Barracks end of the Park, I found it hideous & have been obliged to alter it & take a new line, which will not be so handsome, but it will be far better for building purposes. This will be my final alteration I believe. With this new line I meet every objection, but that of superior effect and beauty on the first line."

There are just two further entries in the Duke's Diaries concerning the Park; the first is for 13th March 1847. In Nottingham for the Assizes the Duke used the occasion to visit the Park. "I had a walk in the Park & made a survey of what had been done, & found many things done of which I had no knowledge. My steward Wilmot has been playing many awkward tricks, & I fear that he is little better than a rascal." The second, for the 3rd July 1847, refers to a meeting in Nottingham with Thomas Winter "who looks after all my building & local concerns here." "I find that the schemes, which we had in view here will not be improvements & that [there is nothing to (?)] do but to adhere to the original plans." As the Duke only refers once to the architect Thomas Chambers Hine in his Diaries, about Maplebeck Parsonage, (calling him 'Haine'), perhaps the words "looks after my building interests" take on significant meaning. Is it possible that Thomas

Top: This print by J. C. Greenwood of 1850 is one of four that shows the undeveloped Park from the Castle to the Barracks. This pastoral scene sweeps across the site of the later Newcastle Drive. To the right the approach to the Park Tunnel, where work had temporarily been halted, can be seen. (L.S.L.)

Middle: This illustration, taken from W. Fyffe's Rambles Around Nottingham (1856) is a little less rectangular than the earlier Picken drawing, but it could be by the same hand. The site for a church is survives and now the spire of St. Barnabas can be seen on the skyline. (L.S.L.)

Bottom: Two houses of the early 1850s, probably by T. C. Hine on the corners of Western Terrace near the northern entrance to the Park.

A

B

C

D

A selection of work by Hine erected mainly in the late 1850s.
A. The entrance to Castle Grove, a date stone in the arch has the date 1856
B. An impressive picture of a house on Castle Grove, which nestles just below the Castle
C. This house is tucked away in Park Ravine. Its angled Italianate corner windows are a feature of several of Hine's houses on Lenton Road, Castle Grove and 1 South Road.
D. A house on Cavendish Crescent South seen from Lenton Road. There is a possibility that this was once the home of the national politician A. J. Mundella.
E and F Strong sturdy houses on Lenton Road showing decorative diapering - patterns in contrasting brickwork and stone dressing.

E

F

Three of Hine's large, early houses on Newcastle Drive all display very impressive entrances to the street and are quite expansive to the rear. The photographs are taken from Newcastle Terrace, which gives some idea of the earthworks needed to cut Newcastle Drive at a lower level.

The Park Tunnel, below, showing left the steps leading from Upper College Street into the open centre of the tunnel; right is a view through the three sections of the tunnel towards the exit on Derby Road.

Left: The encircled eight pointed star motif seen on many Hine houses

A

B

C

E

D

The flamboyant Nottingham architect Watson Fothergill transposed his forename and family name in 1892. Thus the Park houses by this architect before that date are by Fothergill Watson! Here is a small selection of his work.

A. 7 Lenton Road (1873), one of a pair with No. 5 for the Misses Woods. Rather restrained when compared to his later work but his handling of chamfered bricks, plate tracery, and use of stone gives much to admire.

B. Walton House, 39 Newcastle Drive (1886) sits snugly into one of the awkward corner plots that remained to the 1880s. This rear view faces the drop down into Tattershall Drive

C. and D. 3 South Road, one of the largest houses in the Park, was started some time prior to 1880 and was extended in the late1890s. There is far too much here to encompass in one photograph with even more of interest in a 'Baronial' style facing onto Clumber Road South

E. A rear view of a late Fothergill pair on Huntingdon Drive. Several of the architectural flourishes appearing on his commercial work of the 1890s appear here - notice those 'lidded' dormer windows.

Winter commissioned Hine* as the architect for the next phase of the Park's development taking place in the final years of the 4th Duke, who died on 12th January 1851?

In the late 1840s building work restarted in the Park and it is possible that money realised from the sale of Hafod was set aside for this purpose. **Nos. 5, 7, 9, 11 and 21-23 Park Valley** were built and on **Western Terrace (then Clinton Terrace) Nos. 3-4, 5-6, 7-8, and 9-10 joined the earlier Lincoln Villa.** Thomas Chambers Hine is most likely the architect of some of these houses. If so he attempted to blend Robinson's designs with his own eclecticism; pilasters with ionic capitals, pediments, friezes, cornices and balustrades abound. Most people miss these treasures as they dash in and out of the Park along North Road. A good accurate impression of the Park at that time is conveyed in a set of four views, almost a continuous panorama, of Nottingham Park by C. J. Greenwood published in 1850.

A personal feeling about the state of the infrastructure of the Park at this time is revealed in two letters from Sam Newham written to the Duke in 1849. Newham, a tenant of the Duke's for nearly 18 years, was very aggrieved about the state of the Ropewalk, a street shared by the Duke and the town. In April he writes: "I inquired last week of one of the men at work why he so carefully kept the rammel on one side of Rope Walk Street. He replied: "Oh, we have nothing to do with that part, it belongs to the Duke." During the winter there have been holes sufficient to break the spring on any carriage." In July Newham adds further details: "The road is in a most dangerous state. The servants to the Inclosure Commissioners have cut away and lowered their side of the road, our 15 feet remaining high above the other. I only wish your Grace could see it." The Duke's agents Heming and Winter, with or without Sam Newham's help, appear to have resolved "the subject of the terms upon which the Ropewalk was joined up to the Inclosure Commissioners" not long afterwards.

In June 1850 John Bromley of Derby submitted to the Duke a "Rough Outline of the Valuation of the Extra Parochial Property" and projecting 20 years ahead reckoned £170,540. He noted "As building ground it is difficult to say of what value the Park may eventually be found to be and to deprive this property of its Extra-Parochial rights would I consider depreciate the value Ten Thousand Pounds." His eldest son Lord Lincoln's costly divorce in August 1850 might have caused some additional financial constraints but its immediate effect was lessened when the 4th Duke died and Lincoln succeeded to the title.

The late Duke's animosity towards his son, often publicly displayed, was not lost on the elders of Nottingham. Henry Pelham Fiennes Pelham Clinton 5th Duke of Newcastle was certain to receive a level of co-operation from the Town Council never enjoyed by his father.

The radical *Nottingham Review*, for long a strong critic of the 4th Duke's actions carried a full and thoughtful obituary in its issue of 15th January 1851. The writer recalled the effect the eventual passing of the Great Reform Act of 1832 had on the Duke. *He supported with infinitely greater fervour the party that opposed the Reform Act, that memorable statute, which stripped his Grace of borough property, the money value of which in the palmy days of Toryism, have been set down at less than £150,000. He himself estimated it at £200,000.*

The obituary noted the rash acquisitive nature of the Newcastles: *Nothing can be more certain than that his ancestors and he expended large sums in maintaining their Parliamentary interest - a mode of applying capital which, combined with some not very fortunate purchases of land, placed the Duke at an advanced period of his life, in circumstances, by no means easy as regards his pecuniary affairs... for it is very generally understood that whatever inconveniences he may have suffered in matters of finance, it had not been occasioned by profusion or ostentation, but on the contrary, was to be imputed to purchases of land far exceeding in value the amount of capital he could command.*

*For an outline of Hine's career see the Civic Society's T. C. Hine, Architect of Victorian Nottingham

Finally mellowing, the *Review* placed the Duke kindly in an historic context. *Peer that his private virtues will be remembered and admired when his political errors are forgotten; that his character, as an amiable, honourable, high spirited English gentleman will be appreciated when the prejudices and intolerance of the old anti-Catholic Tory will be no longer formidable or offensive.*

Strangely the obituary made no mention of the intended development of the Park into an estate, which had the Duke lived to see it would have been indeed "a means of supplying his exhausted treasury".

The new Duke, the Fifth Duke of Newcastle, was widely known as the very able politician Lord Lincoln, the hereditary title given to the eldest son of the Dukes of Newcastle. On succeeding to the title after the death of his father in January 1851 he entered the 'Other House' and had to part from his close friends in the Commons. There he had made his mark as one of the distinguished younger Peelites, along with W.E. Gladstone and Sidney Herbert. Because of his alienation from his own father, it was said that Sir Robert Peel was more like a father to Lincoln and thereby was possibly being groomed for the Tory leadership; he was certainly highly regarded by several of the leading Tories. Outside politics, Lincoln became a friend of Prince Albert and Queen Victoria.

Three factors in the late 1840s severely hampered Lincoln's true potential: his recurring ill health, the failure of his marriage through his wife's frequent misconduct and the continuing differences with his father. In particular 1850 proved to be a bad year for him, for besides the final illness of his father and the dissolution of his marriage, Sir Robert Peel died.

Lord Lincoln first entered Parliament as the unopposed Tory member for South Nottinghamshire in December 1832. Along with other young progressive Tories including his friend from Oxford days W.E. Gladstone, he was taken up by Sir Robert Peel, forming after 1846 the nucleus of the 'Peelites', those in a divided Conservative Party who supported Peel's policy of free trade.

In 1841 with the return of Peel's government Lincoln was appointed Commissioner for Roads and Forests, a post that brought him into contact with the Royal Family. In 1845 he joined Peel's cabinet.

Early in 1846 he was moved to become Secretary for Ireland, a post he held for a very short time as Peel resigned after the Tory party split following his repeal of the Corn Law Act of 1815. In the resulting election Lincoln, as a supporter of Peel and the free trade movement, lost his South Nottinghamshire seat to the Tory protectionist candidate Thomas B.T. Hildyard who was heavily supported financially by the Duke of Newcastle, as ever the old style ultra Country Tory. This move obviously widened the gulf between father and son.

After some extensive searching a new seat was found for Lincoln: Falkirk, which was narrowly won in the spring of 1846; his liberal tendencies outweighing the imposition of his candidature on the local electorate.

The Tories, now more frequently called Conservatives, were out of office until February 1852 when the Earl of Derby briefly headed a minority government, which lasted until December. Later that month the Earl of Aberdeen formed a Whig-Peelite coalition government in which the Duke of Newcastle was appointed as Secretary of State for War and the Colonies.

Initially the Aberdeen ministry met with general widespread public approval, at least until the outbreak of the Crimean War on 28th March 1854. Thereafter this support soon lessened, progressing quickly to hostility as the country blamed Aberdeen for the mismanagement of the war, forcing him to resign in January 1855. He was succeeded by Viscount Palmerston leading, again, a Whig - Peelite coalition.

Newcastle was responsible for the army, which had not taken part in any European conflict since Waterloo in 1815. Successive governments had limited their expenditure on 'modernising' the armed forces. Thus he inherited an army that was lacking in numbers, poorly equipped, had limited medical support and with no logistical set-up to transport men, equipment and supplies to the far side of Europe.

Newcastle made considerable efforts to rectify most of these shortcomings. He was deliberately hampered by the military establishment. For example he wanted promotion by ability and not by seniority or social standing.

In June 1854 as part of military reform the decision was made to separate the two parts of Newcastle's office. Newcastle opted to retain the post of Secretary of State for War with Sir George Grey taking over as the Secretary of State for the Colonies.

As detailed reports on the conduct of the war and the appalling conditions endured by the British troops in the Crimea reached Britain and were widely circulated, so the public perception of the incompetence of Aberdeen's government and Newcastle in particular became firmly fixed.

The government laboured on for the rest of the year against increasing national criticism often heightened by reports and leaders in *The Times*. The final blow came early in the New Year when John Robuck, the Sheffield M.P. proposed a Committee of Inquiry to investigate the conduct of the war. Lord John Russell, President of the Council, in effect the Leader of the House of Commons, resigned not wishing to defend the ministry. On 29 January 1855 Robuck's proposition was carried by 157 votes. Aberdeen resigned the next day, taking the decision as a vote of no confidence.

Aberdeen formally announced the end of his ministry to the House of Lords in an impassioned speech, in which he declared:

An impartial inquiry, I believe, will fully establish that no indifference has existed to the wants of our army in the Crimea, or any absence of exertion in preparing for the supply of those wants and for promoting the efficiency of its condition. That, I believe, will be the result of an impartial inquiry into this subject; and especially I must consider that my noble Friend, the noble Duke near me (the Duke of Newcastle), has met with great injustice. It is my conviction that his conduct, the more it is inquired into, will be found marked by a degree of assiduity and labour, attention and interest for the duties of his office, which has never been exceeded, nor indeed can be. My Lords, I am not at all surprised at the feeling which generally prevails throughout the country. The public, although they may not always reason justly, yet always feel deeply and strongly.

In an unprecedented move the Duke of Newcastle chose to speak after Aberdeen. He endeavoured, successfully judging by subsequent reports, to reassure the House of his full commitment to the war effort, even though at times he encountered mounting difficulties.

My Lords, various accusations are made against me, of which one of the most prominent is that of incapacity. My Lords, I am the last man who ought to express any opinion on that point. I am ready to leave that in the hands of others, perfectly conscious of many defects. I know that this charge of incapacity is with the public a favourite explanation of every political misfortune; and whether it may be peculiarly justified in my case, or may be attributable to the cause to which I have referred, I leave to the verdict of others. But, my Lords, another charge has been made against me - a charge which I confess I have felt deeply, and which I continue to feel. I have been charged with indolence and indifference. My Lords, as regards the charge of indolence, I have only to say that the public have had, at all events, every hour and every minute of my time. Not one hour of recreation or of amusement have I presumed to think I was entitled to take. My Lords, the other charge that of indifference, is still more painful to me. Indifference my Lords - to what? Indifference to the honour of the country - indifference to the success and to the safety of our army! My Lords, I have myself, like many who listen to me, two dear hostages for my interest in the welfare of the military and naval services of the country to allow of such a sentiment. I have two sons engaged in those two services, and that alone, I think, would be sufficient to prevent me from being indifferent.

Many a sleepless night I have passed, my Lords, thinking over the evils which the public think and say I could have cured; and which, God knows, I would have cured if it had been within my power. Indolence and indifference are not charges that can truly be brought against me. I deny the charges; and I trust that my countrymen will before long be satisfied, whatever they think of my capacity, that there is no ground for fixing this unjust stigma upon me.

In that manner the Duke of Newcastle left office. Lord Palmerston formed the next ministry, once again a Whig - Peelite government. Lord Panmure, a tough talking Scot with the experience of some twelve years military service, was appointed Secretary of State for War on 8th February 1855, overseeing the conduct of the war until peace was agreed through the Treaty of Paris 28th February -30th March 1856. Panmure remained in office until February 1858.

It was later revealed that Lord Russell had first criticised Newcastle's incompetence in a letter to the Earl of Aberdeen in October 1854, stressing the urgent need for a change of unimaginative personnel. In a later letter Russell indicated "I wish, however, that before you decide you should show my letter to the Duke of Newcastle. It was my intention in writing the letter to avoid throwing any blame upon him. Indeed, I think he deserves very great credit for the exertions he has made. But he has not had the authority requisite for so great a sphere, and has not been able to do all that might have been done with larger powers of control."

It is remarkable that against such important affairs of state the serious development of the Park Estate restarted. On 12th January 1854 Thomas Chambers Hine, now the best and busiest of the architects in Nottingham went to London to meet the architect Philip Hardwick, an advisor to the Duke of Newcastle. He returned to Nottingham two days later after being offered and accepting the 'Surveyship of the Park Estate' at a salary of £150 per annum.

This was not the end of Newcastle's political career. He had been admitted as a Privy Councillor in 1841and then in 1860 he became a Knight of the Garter. He joined Lord Palmerston's Liberal administration as Secretary of State for the Colonies in 1859, serving with some distinction until forced to resign through progressive ill health on 2nd April 1864. In just over six months, on 18th October 1864 the Fifth Duke of Newcastle died at Clumber aged 53 years.

Locally the 5th Duke was appointed Lord Lieutenant of Nottinghamshire in 1857 and held the post until his death. His last prominent act in the town was the laying of the foundation stone of the School of Art, Waverley Street on 22nd October 1863.

7. The 5th Duke, Mr. T. C. Hine and the Tunnel Completed

The Nottingham Town Council's expectation of a better relationship with the new Duke, compared with that of his father, was soon proved to be correct. When the town was en fête for the formal opening of the Arboretum on 11th May 1852, the Duke allowed free access to the Castle grounds for locals and visitors.

Before long a more thorough development of the Park was being actively considered, probably sometime in 1853. The preparation of the details within the Parliamentary Bill referred to below would have taken several months. To what extent T.C. Hine was aware of these proposals when he travelled to London to meet with the architect Philip Hardwick is a matter of conjecture.

Barely three weeks later on Friday 5th February 1854, the radical *Nottingham Review* broke the news: *On Wednesday morning, the operation of cutting and paring the surface of portions of Nottingham Park, the property of his Grace the Duke of Newcastle, but from time immemorial open to the public for air, exercise and recreation, was commenced by means of the plough turf cutters ... We have not yet seen the plans but the chief feature of the operations hitherto developed, presents . . . on the west side of the Park a grand square, with a fine site in its centre for a church . . . the other principal streets appear to radiate north and south, the former street line being continued by means of tunnelling into the Derby Road. According to notices, which we understand have been published, a bill will be brought into Parliament, about the 15th instant, promoted by*

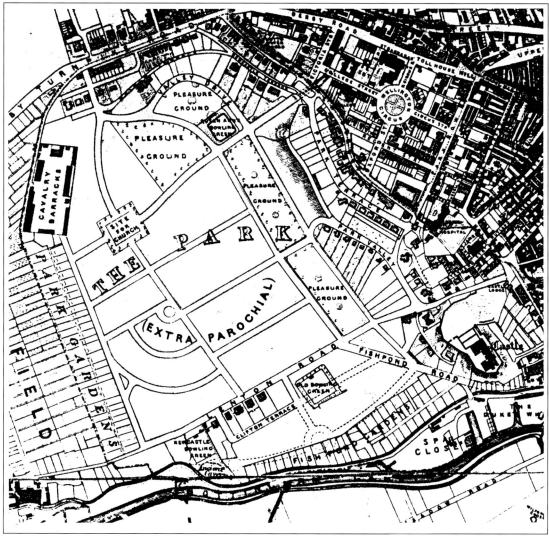

Frederick Jackson's map of Nottingham, published in 1861, was surveyed 1851-61. It shows the layout of the Park more or less as originally intended. There is a site for a church, although who first proposed this is unknown, certainly not Robinson. The road pattern is still rather "rectangular" and the eastern side has a sequence of Pleasure Grounds. The early Hine buildings are shown but there appears to be no attempt to be up to date, for example the Old Bowling Green on Lenton Road is drawn in place.

St. James, Standard Hill The persistence on Jackson's map of a site for a church is strange as nearby on Standard Hill was the church of St. James designed by William Stretton, which opened in 1808. (Demolished 1936).

A

(PROPOSED)

BILL

For Paving, Lighting, Cleansing, Watering, Sewer-
ing, and otherwise Improving and Regulating
the Streets, Squares, and other Places within
the extra-parochial Place called Nottingham
Park, near the Town of Nottingham, and for
other purposes connected therewith.

17 Vict.
Sess. 1854.

FARRER & CO.
66, Lincoln's Inn Fields,
Solicitors.

J. DORINGTON, ELLICOMBES, THOMAS, AND CHALONER SMITH,
Parliamentary Agents,
6, PARLIAMENT STREET.

A

(PROPOSED)

BILL

For Paving, Lighting, Cleansing, Watering, Sewer-
ing, and otherwise Improving and Regulating the
Streets, Squares, and other Places within the
extra-parochial Place called Nottingham Park,
near the Town of Nottingham, and for other
purposes connected therewith.

(The words printed in *Italics* are proposed to be inserted in Committee.)

WHEREAS the Most Noble Henry Pelham, Duke of Newcastle,
claims to be entitled to the freehold and inheritance of the extra-
parochial place called Nottingham Park, near the town of Nottingham, and the other extra-parochial places forming part of the estate at or near
5 the town of Nottingham aforesaid, held with the Castle of Nottingham, including the places known as Spa Close, the Duke's Wharf, and the Castle and
precincts, and the King's Meadows; And whereas several houses and other
buildings have been erected and built, and other houses and buildings are in
the course of erection, and streets and other places are formed and being
10 formed in the said extra-parochial places, and it is in contemplation to build
and make other streets, roads, squares, crescents, terraces, and rows of houses
in the said extra-parochial places; And whereas it would be of great convenience and advantage to the owners and occupiers of houses on the said
estate, and also of public advantage, if a body of Commissioners were ap-
15 pointed and incorporated for paving, lighting, cleansing, watering, and other-
A   wise

Cover and first page of the proposed, but never implemented, Parliamentary Bill entitled 'NOTTINGHAM PARK IMPROVEMENT' (N.U.M.D. Ne C 13459)

This is part of Hine's 'Account with the Duke of Newcastle', from 30 December 1854 to 30 June 1855, which includes work on the Park tunnel. (NUMS) his Grace the Duke of Newcastle, for effecting these improvements as a public undertaking, under the existing Commissioners with the addition of three others to be nominated by his Grace. The general cost of the improvements will be defrayed by a loan of £10,000 repayable by yearly instalments, in thirty years...

The rather conservative *Nottingham Journal* reported on 12 February 1854:

NOTTINGHAM PARK - *Most of our readers are aware that vigorous efforts are now being made to convert the Park and adjacent lands belonging to his grace the Duke of Newcastle to more profitable uses for the duke's benefit. The estate has been mapped out, and roads, squares, terraces and other divisions are being set out with an activity which shows that the parties directing it are in earnest.*

The turf has been removed by the plough from the surface of the lines of the principal streets, which are wide and spacious, and the general design begins now to develop itself. This measure has long been anticipated, and feeble efforts have from time to time during several years past have been made to carry it out. All previous attempts, however, have broken down. Now the matter seems likely to go on.

Some have pretended to be overwhelmed with grief at the proposed profitable and judicious use of the Park, but we confess we do not participate in their sorrow. Civilisation is better than barbarism, and cultivation has more charms for us than the briars and thorns of unassisted nature. The Park, to our mind, will be much improved to the public by the intended appropriation of it. Even the removal of the turf from the intended roads has benefitted rather than injured its appearance from the higher grounds, and when it becomes dotted over with mansions, villas, terraces, and squares, each surrounded with ornamental inclosures filled with trees, shrubs, and flowers, it will present... the most lovely landscape possible to conceive. It will afford us as much fresh air, pleasant walking, and more enchanting scenery than ever.

The 5th Duke certainly intended to bring the Park's development to fruition. J. Dorrington and Co. had been appointed as Parliamentary agents and they prepared "Nottingham Park Estate District Improvement. A Proposed bill" (17 VICT SESS 1854). A "proposed bill" is usually a notice of intent circulated in the area of the intended action; therefore it is not surprising to find the bill was not presented to either House. It is doubtful that the Duke's finances could augment the loan of £10,000 to any great extent. In fact, from his limited resources, during the years 1854-9 the Duke 'invested' £70,000 in Shireoaks Colliery in the hope of striking a rich coal seam.

Under the Bill twelve local Commissioners were appointed: Jonathan Reckless, then currently the Mayor of Nottingham; John Bradley; Francis Braithwaite; Joseph Braithwaite; Hugh Bruce Campbell; Robert Cooke; William Felkin; John Heard; Thomas Herbert; Edward Munk; Samuel Newham; John Thackeray. All were "inhabitants within the limits of this Act". In fact seven of the Commissioners resided on the Ropewalk, and one each lived on Park Row, Park Terrace, Derby Terrace and Western Terrace. Only Cooke lived outside the limits of the Park. The list included six past or future Mayors of Nottingham. Six were in the lace trade, three in hosiery, two were styled "proprietors" and there was one solicitor.

The first three special Commissioners were John Parkinson, Solicitor of Lincoln's Inn Fields, London, Philip Hardwick, Architect R.A. of Cavendish Square, London and John Bromley of Derby, Surveyor and Agent for the Dukes of Newcastle.

The Parliamentary Act which would follow the proposed Bill was to be known as The Nottingham Park Improvement Act. Rather surprisingly, considering that the newspapers' reports had indicated work had started, it was stated within the Bill that it would *come into operation on the First Thursday of September, One thousand eight hundred and fifty-four.*

However as the Bill was never put before Parliament there must be some doubt about whether the Commissioners ever had any direct input or influence on the early stages of the development of the Park Estate. The account in the *Review* did however refer to *existing commissioners*, a mention that adds to the puzzle.

The appointment of Thomas Chambers Hine was a shrewd move, at this time he was the best and most successful of the local architects. The 1850s was to be his great decade. He had already been responsible for a wide range of domestic and commercial buildings including some fine houses, among them his own, 25 Regent Street in the Derby Road Lammas Fields area adjoining the Park. Commercially he was currently restyling the Lace Market area.

T.C. Hine, with his assistant Robert Evans, changed the concept of the Park, from the angular layout, including a site for a church, shown on Jackson's plan (1851-61) to the crescents and circuses of Salmon's plan (also 1861). Jackson's detailing might be correct up to c.1859 but Salmon's map, whilst displaying roads not yet constructed, is very close to the architects' eventual road pattern. This radical change of layout is very puzzling. One possibility might lie in the dedications of the plans. Jackson's dedication is: *To The Right Worshipful THE MAYOR, Aldermen and Common Council of Nottingham,* while Salmon dedicates his plan: *To the Most Noble Henry Pelham Clinton, Duke of Newcastle, K. G. &c, Lord Lieutenant of the County.* Perhaps in this way Salmon was thanking the Duke for some insight into Hine's intentions!

Hine set to work completing the Park Tunnel, which he saw as an integral part of a substantial road construction project in the eastern and northern parts of the Park. For his major new road Hine excavated some 15ft. of the natural slope below Newcastle Terrace so that even the tallest of any intended houses would in no way obstruct the views enjoyed by the residents of the Ropewalk. (Access to the rear of the Ropewalk houses was from (Upper) Newcastle Terrace). This new road, now Newcastle Drive, was constructed in two portions, Lower Newcastle Terrace and Pelham Terrace. Lower Newcastle Terrace sloped away from the end of Park Terrace, crossed the line of the tunnel, levelled out, then climbed up to Derby Road west of Canning Circus, whilst Pelham Terrace branched off this line and ran below and parallel to Derby Road to link up with North Road. Linking the different levels of Upper and Lower Newcastle Terrace was a buttressed brick wall which lasted until the mid 1980s when it was decided that an extensive replacement was needed.. Legend has it that Hine engaged railway 'brickies' to construct these buttresses.

Fragments of Hine's accounts for this phase, January to June 1855, survive. J. and F. Loverseed were the main contractors who received almost £3,000 ". . . on account of Tunnel and Roads" between autumn 1854 and Christmas 1855. The Park Tunnel was almost complete by 11th May 1855. That evening the achievement was celebrated at the Milton's Head, Derby Road, where the workmen involved were treated to a supper and "sumptuous entertainment" at the Duke's expense of £5! Hine's assistant, managing clerk Robert Evans, chairing the proceedings, *complimented the workmen upon their general good behaviour, and expressed his satisfaction at their having arrived at this advanced stage of the works without any serious accident.* He proposed the usual loyal toasts and the health of his Grace the Duke of Newcastle, and that of Mr. Hine and Messrs. J. and F. Loverseed were drunk with all due honours. It was clear that *Harmony and good feeling characterised the proceedings of the evening. At eleven o'clock the company broke up, highly delighted with the entertainment.* (*Nottingham Journal,* 18 May 1855). Evans became a partner in 1857.

On his magnificent Birkin Building (1855) on Broadway in the Lace Market, Hine employed Garland and Holland (G. and H.); and he also employed them for "Centering the Tunnel Arch", paying them £62-10-0d. Hine's account sheet also has details of the cost of landscaping of the tunnel and its approaches. The planting of trees and shrubs was carried out by Mr. Pearson of Chilwell. The shrubs came from his extensive nurseries, and the larger trees were from the Castle's plantations. J Holmes, stonemason, was paid £60 "on account of quoins and arch stones of tunnel". On the credit side just over £36 was raised by the sale of Park turf to several customers including the Church Cemetery (£18) and the Nottingham Hospital (£1-17-8d).

Fyfe in his book *Rambles Round Nottingham* (1856) gives facts about the tunnel which he might well have obtained from the description given in either the *Journal* or the *Nottingham Review* issues of 18 May 1855. Briefly, the entrance to the tunnel from Derby Road is a roadway 33ft wide, College Street is spanned by a semi-skew arch 27ft high and 23ft clear breadth. The main tunnel is cut from solid Bunter sandstone; horse-shoe shaped, it is some 80 yards long with height and width approximately that of the arch. On the Park side the roadway spreads out to a width of 50ft. The pedestrian entrance to the tunnel was via a spiral staircase of 96 broad steps of York stone, divided into five flights of stairs round a concealed shaft at the top of College Street. A pedestrian entry might appear strange for a carriage way into a potential high class residential district. Here a glance at Jackson's map - often lightly dismissed - should explain all. At this time it was intended to have a range of Pleasure Grounds in the valley of the Park. In fact the *Journal* enthused: *We are glad to learn that it is probable that a large space of land east and west in the hollow will be laid out as pleasure grounds.* Although the "Grounds" were never laid out in the manner suggested, this is the area now given to tennis and bowls.

Some resentment about the loss of the Park's amenities still persisted, yet when *the new approach from Derby Road to the Park was thrown open to the public during Sunday 20th May (1855)... it was perambulated by several thousand pedestrians.* The earlier account in the *Review* noted: *We believe that His Grace in passing through the tunnel the other day, bestowed upon it his highest approval and even the warmest encomiums.* Pedestrians still find the tunnel a boon; it provides a quick escape from the bustle of Derby Road to the peaceful bowl of the Park. Over a hundred and fifty years on it remains an impressive, ingenious and picturesque solution to a problem never really set.

The gradient of the tunnel is about 1 in 12, steeper than the intended 1 in 14. There is no record of a carriage actually using the tunnel, though no doubt there was some form of trial on completion. A drawing in *The Architect* October 2 1880 does rather fancifully show a carriage and pair entering the tunnel from the Park side. Allen's *Handbook to Nottingham 1866* revealed: *In 1844 a road was formed to communicate with Derby Road by means of a tunnel, but the latter has not yet been made available.* Delay in building in the heart of the Park made its use almost pointless, as easier routes were then available. Entry and exit via North Road avoided Canning Circus; routes along Lenton Road and Fishpond Gardens skirting the base of the Castle rock avoided the centre of the town if the destination was the railway station or Trent Bridge.

By c.1859 Hine had built **nos. 1-3, 5, 7, 11-13, 29 and 31-33 Newcastle Drive; no.35 came a little later**. The value of these houses is given in a letter of 18 November 1856 to Alexis Baillon who had a plot of 2,106 yards: "When completed to the adopted design I consider that your house in Newcastle Terrace (now Drive) will be worth £3,000 . . ." **Clinton Terrace** on Derby Road was designed by Hine to form with Robinson's **Derby Terrace** a northern boundary wall to the Park.

Across the Park Hine was building on the Lenton Road. Early in the work, in October 1856 there was a problem of finance. A worried Philip Hardwick had written to the Duke: "As little as possible has been done for some time past and only work commenced early this year completed..." An extra £1,000 was needed to pay contractors, money which was due the previous month. The Castle Hill houses on **Castle Grove, dated 1856,** were under construction, and three families were in residence by 1858. Except for No. 1 and 3 Hine developed **Lenton Road from the Western end, nos. 33, 31, 30, 29, 28, 27 and 25 were built before the Old Bowling Green disappeared c. 1858. Nos. 23, 19, 17, 15 and 13 Lenton Road and no. 1 Clifton Terrace/Park Ravine were completed before 1861.** In May 1859 Hine wrote to Hardwick giving his intention ". . . to commence on the metalling and servicing of Lenton Road by October next". A cautious attempt was made to build away from the periphery; before Salmon's map was published in 1861 **no. 1 South Road and nos. 13, 15, 19 and 21 Cavendish Crescent South** were erected. No. 19 was the residence of A. J. Mundella, then of the hosiers Hine & Mundella and later an influential M.P.

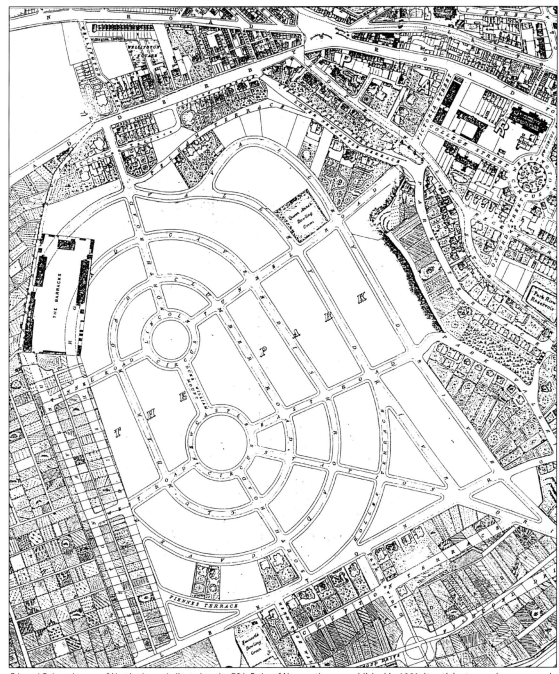

Edward Salmon's map of Nottingham, dedicated to the fifth Duke of Newcastle, was published in 1861. It anticipates, or shows, so much of the eventual layout of the Park that the cartographer must have had access to Hine and Evans' revised plans. Very few houses were added to those shown before 1870.

This drawing of the approach to the Park tunnel appeared in Allen's Handbook to Nottingham, prepared in conjunction with the visit of the British Association for the Advancement of Science in 1866. The temporary abandonment of the development of the Park is all too apparent.

A

B

C

D

E

Later Hine Houses

A. No.1. Duke William Mount (1870s) displays an impressive use of brickwork with stone dressing and has an overall gothic feel. The central feature from the entrance to the shaped gable is worthy of serious attention. A cover photograph shows an intriguing side elevation.

B. Mevell House, 7 Newcastle Circus, another house of the 1870s is said to be in the architect's 'mature classical' style

C. & D. Both of these contrasting houses on Lenton Avenue are seen from Hardwick Road. On Lenton Avenue the houses have been built so that their fronts face their rear gardens and the Park. The plainer rear elevations, 'tradesmen's entrances', line Lenton Avenue.

E. This pair of more modestly designed houses on the Lenton Road - Park Drive corner is part of the later quality infill.

F. 19 Park Terrace of 1881, recently partially re-numbered, is the last of Hine's grand Park houses. Prominently, precariously perched over the Park Tunnel, the house has a plaque carrying the date and initials T.C.H. as well as several of Hine's distinctive eight pointed star air vents.

F

Top
Much of the Park can be seen in this seasonal photograph of the Park taken from the roof of the castle. On the left skyline is Peveril Tower (c.1875) on Cavendish Crescent North, now almost hidden by trees at ground level. To the right are the rear elevations of the Park Terrace houses. The line of Park Valley and the start of Lenton Road can be followed. It is possible, with care to pick out individual houses; in the left hand corner is the rear of the 1873 pair by Fothergill Watson. (Photograph by Martine Hamilton Knight)

Bottom pair
Most of the modern housing in the Park has been rather insipid, driven by location rather than design. One exception is the work by local architects Marsh - Grochowski. Their 'One Degree West' on Western Terrace the most imposing of recent houses in the Park, perhaps in Nottingham, follows one of the Park's traditions of having the more impressive façade to the rear. (Photographs by Martine Hamilton Knight).

The Council, when necessary, worked amicably with the Duke. For example on 20 November 1854 the Council agreed, subject to certain conditions, to sell land to the west of Canal Street to the Duke of Newcastle for the "purpose of making a road from the Park into Canal Street." A Council Committee on public footpaths in the Park was set up in 1857 to negotiate a new route for the traditional Micklethorn Jury through the Castle Yard, and the Duke agreed to alter some of his new roads. On 9 November 1857 it was resolved in Council to thank the Duke of Newcastle and Earl Manvers, the major land owner in Sneinton, "for their constant and active interest in the Institutions of …Nottingham," and their readiness to promote local as well as public and national interests.

About this time the Council received a letter from the Secretary of War, saying that as the Barracks belonging to the Duke of Newcastle were needed by him, the troops there must leave Nottingham, unless a new Barrack was provided. If the Council would provide a site, Government would provide a building. As noted later, this move was a little premature.

The various branches of the Newcastle family and their possessions, as well as the cardinal points, provided Hine with a generous supply of road names, and as the new roads were being laid out so they were planted with the Siberian elms which later became a feature of the Park.

8. The Later Stages of developing the Park Estate

As suggested, Edward Salmon must have either consulted Hine or had access to his master plan for the Park; for the dumb bell of Lincoln Circus - Duke William Mount - Newcastle Circus, surrounded by a series of crescents joined by parallel drives, are all carefully drawn in on his plan of 1861. Most were built within the decade; only a fragment of an extra road, East Road, was built as Clare Valley. Valley Drive was conceived as a long sweeping road but in fact was constructed in two detached parts, Tennis Drive and Huntingdon Drive. The less attractive area to the south was left until after the diversion of the River Leen and the formation of Lenton (Castle) Boulevard in 1883-4. Through the line of the Western Park Gardens Lenton Avenue is tentatively marked out leading up to the side of the Barracks.

The 60-year lease of the Barracks expired at Michaelmas 1853 but the lease was extended for a further 5 years at the increased annual rental of £500. A break in the tenancy allowed the rent to rise to £550 on renewal. In March 1858 the War Office re-negotiated with Philip Hardwick for further yearly renewals at an annual rent of £750 until the Barracks were finally relinquished on Lady Day 1861.

The *Nottingham Date Book* records that on 30 May 1860 the 11th Hussars left the Nottingham Barracks, "which were not afterwards permanently occupied." Had there been any urgency to implement Hine's proposals, no doubt the Barracks would have been demolished later in 1861. However, rooms in the empty Barracks were let out occasionally and accounted as casual rents until 1865. Various open air events were held in the Barrack Yard by travelling showmen; the demonstration given by the famous French tightrope walker, Blondin, on 30th July 1861 was particularly popular. Drill parades were held on the old Barrack Square by various companies of the expanding Robin Hood Rifles until 1881, by which time the buildings of the Barracks had been demolished some ten years.

Lenton Avenue never did sweep around to North Road. A right-angled bend takes it to Alexander Road, whilst its intended curve, now Pelham Crescent, became a cul-de-sac.

All except five of some 60 houses shown in the hollow of the Park on Salmon's map lie on the periphery. Tarbotton's map of 1877, the next reliable map available, has approximately another 70 houses. Street directories are available for the years between, but, because few Park houses were then named or numbered, and some roads were re-named, and because some families moved within the Park, determining growth is difficult if not unreliable. A rough estimate would give no more than 25 new houses in the decade 1861-71. In the 1860s the only new roads to have buildings were Park Drive (Salmon's Station Drive) and Holles Crescent; Newcastle Drive is first named in 1867.

The British Association met in Nottingham in 1866 and Allen's *Handbook to Nottingham*, compiled with this gathering in mind, pointed out: *Some years since the Park was portioned out for building purposes, and, to some extent, has been restricted in consequence, it has also been mutilated by the formation of unfinished roads...The princely residences surrounding the Park give an air of grandeur and dignity, and help to compensate for the now unfinished appearance of the estate generally...*

Twice in December 1867 William Ewart Gladstone, the eminent Liberal politician and one of the 5th Duke's executors, accompanied by Mr. F. Ouvry, estate solicitor, visited Nottingham and met with Hine. On the 2 December, after visiting the Lace Market their brief tour ended with a walk through the Park "to see the improvements, which are being carried out on this portion of the late Duke of Newcastle's estate." Later Hine recalled that during the visit a week later, Gladstone and Ouvry agreed to the formation of Pleasure Grounds in the Park, all three taking lunch at the George Hotel. Within these two reports are hints that the development within the Park had restarted.

Several writers have noted that Notts County Football Club, established formally in December 1864, played its first games on an unknown pitch in the Park Estate. What is more convincing is that the Nottingham Football Club set up in 1862, which became the nucleus of Notts County, played some informal games in the Park Hollow. The early Notts County players included E.B. Steegman, C.S. Wardle, and A.B. Baillon, all connected with the Lace Trade. The Baillon family was one of the earliest residents on Newcastle Drive, which then overlooked an empty Park Hollow; whilst the Steegman family lived in a house backing onto the Ropewalk. Notts County's initial games were played on the Meadows Cricket Ground.

The reasons why building all but stopped are not absolutely clear. Fundamentally the amount of capital needed to sustain development of the inner Park was badly under-estimated. The 5th Duke was broken mentally by the Crimean War; failing health forced him to resign as Colonial Secretary in April 1864 and he died suddenly at Clumber on 18th October 1864, aged 53 years. Investment from Newcastle funds would be temporarily curtailed whilst executors, trustees and outside lawyers endeavoured to sort out settlement, inheritance and even the monetary tangle remaining from the late Duke's expensive 1850 divorce. Many potential residents of the Park had made their money in cotton textiles but from the early 1860s there was a world-wide shortage of cotton due to the American Civil War (1861-5) and its aftermath, which depressed these textile industries. In the latter part of the decade the cotton trade revived and the lace and hosiery 'barons' prospered. Soon many of these industrialists were in such a financial position that commissioning a grand house in the Park was not only possible but desirable.

The death of the 4th Duke in 1851 had not been mentioned in Council, however on 25 October 1864 the Council expressed its sorrow at the death of the 5th Duke of Newcastle, noting that his "noble devotion to public duty...unvarying kindness...generous liberality and...energetic personal promotion of everything which tended towards the social improvement and advantage of this locality have...endeared him to the inhabitants of this Town and neighbourhood."

During the 1870s building proceeded in unhindered bursts, and many of the now familiar roads were developed. In 1871 the Royal Horticultural Society held its inaugural annual exhibition in the Park; Nottingham having been chosen from 50 hopeful towns. The *Nottingham Journal* on 27 June expressed its delight *...it is perhaps the most suitable plot of ground that could have been selected. It is situated at the west end of the town, it is pleasantly surrounded with the houses of the gentry, whose terraced gardens and richly adorned rocky recess are, and have long been, the theme of general admiration.*

Nevertheless over all of these houses loomed the still blackened shell of the Castle. Various schemes for the future use of the Castle were put before the 6th Duke. When Hine presented the Duke with a proposal made by the County magistrates for converting the Castle into a prison and Court of Justice he asked Hine if he thought his father would have approved such a scheme had he been alive. Hine replied: 'No sir, honestly speaking I do not think he would.' To which the Duke replied: 'I will not give it mine.'

In February 1873 the Town Council had appointed a Museum Site Committee to find a permanent location for the Midland Counties Art Exhibition. The Committee reported back in August with the recommendation that the Castle and its grounds be acquired from the Trustees of the late Duke of Newcastle to house the Art Exhibition and Natural History Museum. This was approved and it became incorporated in the Nottingham Improvement Act 1874.

On 10 May 1875 Mr. W.E. Gladstone, a trustee of the Park Estate and Mr. F. Ouvry met with the Mayor, the Vicar of St. Mary's, T.C. Hine as architect to the Park Estate, the Castle Museum Project Committee and others at the Drill Hall at the Castle to examine and discuss plans for the restoration of the castle and its adaptation as a museum. On the following day, 11 May, occurred one of the Park's often recounted events. "Mr. Gladstone felled a tree in the Park 5½ ft. in circumference." Whether it was to impress a lady is a matter of conjecture. A memorial plaque on Tunnel Drive survives, suggesting a more modest size!

The renamed Castle Museum Committee reported in September 1875 that arrangements had been made with the Trustees of the Duke of Newcastle for the lease of Nottingham Castle, and upwards of 25,000 sq.yds. of the surrounding land for 500 years at £40 for the first and second years and thereafter at £200 a year. The estimated cost of the restoration and conversion into a museum was £15,000. The Committee was empowered to obtain plans etc for work. On 17 January 1876 the Castle Museum Committee reported that they had received and approved plans for the restoration of the building and its adaptation as a museum from Messrs. T. C. Hine and Son. The Committee was authorized to obtain tenders. (Son George was promoted after Evans left in 1867).

So between 1876-8 the blackened shell of the Castle was transformed by Hine and Son into the first provincial Museum of Fine Art. The Midland Counties Art Museum was formally opened on 3 July 1878 by His Royal Highness the Prince of Wales, accompanied by Princess Alexandra. The town was impressively bedecked for this royal visit. The final approach to the Castle was through the Park Estate, from Derby Road via Newcastle Circus and Park Drive to the Park Gate. The *Nottingham Date Book* (1884) noted "Beyond what had been done by private residents, no decorations were attempted in the Park, the natural loveliness of which rendered such inadvisable." "In Newcastle Circus there was a large gathering of school children (under nines) of too tender an age to take part in the (earlier) Market Place demonstration."

An anonymous reporter, no doubt covering the visit of the Prince of Wales, wrote a rather sneering piece in the London magazine *Whitehall Review* in the week following the visit entitled *Nottingham Society*. Within a long sarcastic article were the following lines. *Moreover, no one can deny that "The Park", which represents the Belgravia of Nottingham, is a grand site hardly equalled perhaps in England. The houses, however, which on this exquisite site (Nottingham) Society has built for itself, are, with very rare exceptions, unutterably ugly, illustrating with a force which no words can attain how terribly true is John Ruskin's dogma that a people's art but reflects that people's mind.* The whole article was unwisely reprinted in the *Nottingham Journal* and the editor received a barrage of indignant letters including one, which whilst singing the praises of the "Parkers" referred to the original piece as a "foul libel".

The Nottingham Borough Extension Act of 1877 (Section 55) contained "Provision for protection of Nottingham Park Estate" so the continuation of its unique status was assured, and during the 1880s what remained unfulfilled of Hine's plan was steadily achieved. By 1891 relatively few plots remained - some on Cavendish Crescent East and Clumber Road East, and some close to the southern limits, whilst **Huntingdon Drive only had no. 3 and 4, its two Watson Fothergill houses.**

Watson Fothergill (1841-1928)* was the most flamboyant of Nottingham's Victorian architects but he, as well as lesser architects, had to have his plans and materials approved by Hine acting for the Newcastle Estate to maintain the quality of houses erected. Fothergill was responsible for around 30 of the Park houses, his most impressive being the early Gothic pair, **5-7 Lenton Road (1873), nos. 27 (1884) and 39 (Walton House, 1886) Newcastle Drive, the tiled 14 Cavendish Crescent East (c.1896) and the massive and eclectic no. 3 South Road (c.1880 and later).**

* For more details see 'Watson Fothergill Architect', Nottingham Civic Society's Get to Know Nottingham No. 7.

This extract from the Ordnance Survey Map of 1886, which was probably surveyed two or three years earlier, gives an accurate picture of the extent of the Park's development in the early 1880s. For example, Penrhyn House, dated 1879, is shown as is, possibly, 19 Park Terrace of 1881. Whilst there are too many cartographic symbols, no doubt endeavouring to convey the idea that the gardens of the Park's houses had abundant shrubs and trees, careful examination of the map particularly of those undeveloped plots is quite revealing.

In the mid 1980s the original Newcastle Drive butress wall (left) was in poor condition and was replaced (right)

Arthur Marshall (1858-1915), another talented local architect is represented solely but impressively by **Adam House ('Brightlands', 1885, for Samuel Bourne) on Clumber Road East**, which was well received in *The Architect*, 30th October, 1885. Of the minor builder-architects, John Loverseed built much of **Pelham Crescent (1869-74) including his own house; Haddon House, Cavendish Crescent North, and on Holles Crescent (late 1860s). Edwin Loverseed his brother built and lived in Gladstone House (1876).** Henry Daubney erected four attractive houses on Cavendish Crescent North in the late 1880s. James Wright, a prolific builder of much cheaper housing around the town put up houses on the eastern portion of **Cavendish Crescent South. No. 11** was built by Robert Evans for himself, and no. 15 Lenton Road (incorrectly dated 1856) is also alleged to be by Evans. Hine's son George Thomas was the architect for houses on the southern side of Newcastle Circus. A house by Samuel Dutton Walker on **Park Drive** was illustrated in *The Building News*, December 1877.

Hine's own architectural contribution can be considered in two ways: the impressive individual houses and the splendid groupings. The individual houses of note are: **no. 19 Park Terrace (1881), seemingly perched precipitously on the edge of the Tunnel; the commanding Peveril Tower, 9 Cavendish Crescent North (c.1875); no. 1 South Road (c.1859); no. 17 Lenton Avenue (1886) in the Queen Anne style, and Penrhyn House (1879) Clumber Road East. The most varied group must be nos. 1 (Gothic), 2 and 3 (mildly Elizabethan) Duke William Mount with just beyond Mevell House, no. 7 Newcastle Circus (classical), all built by 1881.**

Other houses to savour collectively are **nos. 21-33 Lenton Road (mostly 1858-9), no. 1 Newcastle Drive and the adjoining houses (c.1857 and later) seen from Newcastle Terrace, Castle Grove (1856-8) viewed from Peveril Drive, and the backs of the Western Terrace houses (late 1840s).** Several of Hine's earlier houses have quite distinctive decorative stone features including an eight pointed star within a broad ring; on some later houses he prefers swags and other terra-cotta ornamentation.

In 1890-1 George Hine was appointed Consulting Architect to H.M. Commissioners in Lunacy and moved to London. Thus the ageing and increasingly inactive T. C. Hine decided to retire. He died in 1899 in his 86th year, having lived to see his ambitious plans for the old Castle deer park almost entirely completed. Outsiders found Hine's geometrical layout puzzling, but for residents its maze-like qualities enhanced their privacy.

Before the end of Hine's reign as Park Supremo some of the Pleasure Grounds marked out on the mid-century plans were formally set out. Tennis became a social indulgence. Two tennis clubs were formed: the Newcastle, around 1886 and the Park in 1882, possibly 1880. The Newcastle Club was until 1901 known as the Cavendish. In 1975 the Newcastle, the Park and the younger Tattershall (1963-4) clubs merged to form the Nottingham Club, which was based at the Newcastle courts on Tattershall Drive.

The Castle is prominent above the less dramatic houses in Hope Drive at the Southern end of the Estate

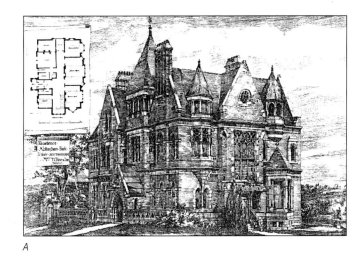

A

C

B

D

These drawings of Park houses and the Park tunnel appeared in the national architectural press.

A. This un-named 'Residence Nottingham Park Estate' by T. C. Hine was published in The Builder 10th January 1885
B. 19 Park Terrace, dated 1881, and the entrance to the Park Tunnel, the illustration appeared in The Architect October 2nd 1880.
The carriage traffic probably existed only in the imagination of the artist.
C. This 'House Nottingham Park' by S. Dutton Walker F.S.A. which was in The Building News 5th October 1877 is on Park Drive. It is now called 'Ashley House'.
D. Arthur Marshall's only house in the Park, 'Brightlands', now 'Adam House' on Clumber Road East, was designed for the industrialist and artist Samuel Bourne. A reproduction of this painting was in The Architect 30th October 1885.

9. Postscript: The Twentieth Century

The great days of the Park Estate continued until the outbreak of war in 1914. From around 1900 the new generation of Nottingham's wealthy businessmen had greater mobility through the acquisition of a motor car and could build their mansions well beyond the City's boundary. After the war the fluctuations of trade and fashion brought a decline in affluence in Nottingham, especially in textiles. In the Park the cost of maintaining the grand houses in the manner expected rose and prospective new tenants were often deterred by the short time remaining on Victorian leases. In the 1930s houses in the Park could be purchased very cheaply; a few were demolished and many were converted into flats, often regrettably not very sympathetically.

The extreme example of the changing fortunes of the Park must be the sale of *St. Helier*, the former home of the then late Lord Trent on 15 June 1932. On the following day the *Daily Guardian* carried the story. *St. Helier*, costing upwards of £6,000 and in a good state of repair, had been unoccupied for some 10 years. The auctioneers Walker, Walton and Hanson considered the building a white elephant and somewhat reluctantly added it to the sale catalogue of the day, with no reserve on the property. At the auction the *St. Helier* item was reached. "When bidding started at £5 there was some laughter, which changed to amazement when the hammer fell at £7." The purchaser, from Wilford, for his outlay of £7 not only got a house with central heating and a lift but also grounds with paved walks, a rose garden and two tennis courts! On the downside an annual ground rent of £116 had to be paid to the Newcastle Office. The newspaper noted that the building could not be pulled down; there were restrictive covenants which made it impossible for any other use.

In 1938 the Park Estate was purchased by the Nuffield Trust who passed it to the Oxford University Chest, for whom it was managed by the London Chartered Surveyors, Chestertons, until 1986.

After the Second World War the decline continued and wartime neglect accentuated an already serious situation. Further insensitive repairs and conversions followed. The motor car as a stationary and moving object added to the Park's problems; ironically several coach houses were converted into desirable residences. Parts of large gardens were sold off for development to help the upkeep of existing houses. There was originally leasehold of 99 years on all properties within the Park Estate but between 1940 and 1986 all of the freeholds had been sold. Several restrictive covenants were retained in order to maintain some degree of control and harmony within the Estate. One of the largest transactions took place in June 1960 when Messrs. Warmington of London auctioned 49 lots of houses in the Park

During the 1960s the City Council flirted inexplicably with the idea of routing a new urban motorway through the heart of the Park. Thankfully common sense prevailed and in 1969 the Council recognised the uniqueness of the Park by designating it a Conservation Area. In 1974 the Department of the Environment followed by pronouncing the Estate a Conservation Area of "outstanding importance in the national context". During the 1970s hope and optimism were backed by a general interest in the fabric of the houses, in many cases then over a hundred years old. New owners brought cash and an enlightened attitude for the loving and careful restoration of their property. Often, in addition, the blight of the 20th Century had first of all to be removed. Now 93 buildings and ancillary features; railings, retaining walls etc and the Park Tunnel are statutorily listed and more should appear on the City Council's Local Interest List when it is revised.

In 1986 agreement was finally reached between the Park Residents Association and the Oxford University Chest. As a result a newly formed company The Park Estate Limited became owners of the Park Estate and in so doing took on the rights and responsibilities of ownership. The Company was limited by guarantee. The Park remained a private estate with the Company taking over the maintenance of the roads, footpaths and common areas. In 1987 the Company took over the gas lighting system. The City of Nottingham converted from gas to electric lighting in 1937 but the survival of the gas lighting from 220 lamp posts in the Park is unique and certainly adds to the charms for the visitor. However residents have mixed feelings for some would prefer change.

When the Community Charge was introduced in the Local Government Finance Act 1988 abolishing the rating system, the existing arrangement for funding the Company ceased. As a result it became necessary for the Company to promote a Parliamentary Bill. This, The Nottingham Park Estate Bill approved by Parliament, became law in April 1990. Thus the Nottingham Park Estate Limited, a private company limited by guarantee was established now with the legal powers to raise funds for the Park Estate.

Once the transfer of responsibilities from the Oxford University Chest were completed, the new Company decided its priorities: to improve the roads and footpath surfaces; reduce parking dramatically by unauthorised users; reduce the volume of through traffic (motorists using The Park as a shortcut) and generally improve the amenities within The Park Estate. Section 14 of the Nottingham Park Estate Act 1990 sets out the powers given to the Company for stopping up roads and traffic regulations.

Today the Park Estate remains visibly a distinctive Victorian creation, country acres "near to Nottingham". Formerly once a year on the last Thursday before Christmas, the Park gates were closed, as a practical gesture to remind outsiders of the Park's private status but this has been discontinued for a number of years. Telephone wires are discreetly underground. From the outset the 5th Duke promised his tenants a life "free from any annoyance whatsoever" and the earliest leases contained covenants against businesses of any kind being established or conducted in the Park. Other restrictions were added progressively for the common good.

In its heyday, before the First World War, in the 154 acres of the Park Estate were 355 houses. Today there are some 450 houses and about 700 flats, many formed through conversion of the older large houses. The population is approaching 2,000. In recent years there have been a number of modern houses erected. For some folk, even with those houses in harmony there is a sense of intrusion, exceptions are those by Marsh and Grochowski.

Prominent among the Victorian residents were national figures: Jesse Boot, A. J. Mundella, John Player; and a considerable number of families prominent in the commercial and administrative life of the town. Edward Goldschmidt J.P., industrialist, Mayor 1881 and 1889: Sir Samuel Johnson, Town Clerk: Thomas Forman J.P., printer: John Manning J.P., grocer: Samuel Bourne J.P., cotton doubler and pioneering photographer are typical and represent many manufacturers, specialist tradesmen, solicitors and engineers; it is a long list. Mention must be made that the early years of Captain Albert Ball V.C. were spent in the Park; appropriately his memorial statue by Henry Poole is located nearby in the Castle Grounds.

In recent years for many people, resident and non-resident, part of the Park has reverted to its original intention as a recreational area. There are two bowling clubs, one the Queen Anne, now on Duke William Mount, was formed in 1856; the County Tennis Courts, established in 1931, became for a time in the 1970s the home of John Player Tournament. The Squash Courts house the Nottingham Squash Club, one of Britain's premier clubs. Not all of the notable sporting events are of recent date. One of the greatest took place in July 1913 when a semi-final of the Davis Cup was played out on the Newcastle Courts. Under the rules of the day the semi-final winners played each other for the right to challenge the holders, in 1913 the British Isles. America beat Germany 3-0 in the Park, whilst Canada overcame Belgium in Folkestone. America subsequently was victorious over Canada and then challenged and defeated the holders. One of the Americans is said to have smashed and bounced a return into Clare Valley!

The creation of such an estate had its critics, from the horror expressed in the 1820s at the mere thought of development, through the attacks on the idyllic life style of its residents and the concentration of such affluence so close to the slums of the lower part of the town, right through to the anti-conservationists of the 1960s.

The twists of fate that influenced the interaction of the Newcastle family, its estates, and the Council and inhabitants of Nottingham, happily brought together the 5th Duke of Newcastle and Thomas Chambers Hine. The perception and vision of this partnership created the feeling of a compact country estate and presented Nottingham with a legacy without a parallel in England.

ACKNOWLEDGEMENTS

I wish to thank the staffs of the Manuscript Department University of Nottingham, the Local Studies Library, Angel Row, Nottingham, the Nottinghamshire County Record Office and the City of Nottingham Planning Department. The late Keith Train, Alan Cameron and Stephen Best were always encouraging and willing to listen and discuss ideas for the first edition. For this second edition Alan Bates, Stephen Best and Richard Gaunt have always been extremely helpful. Richard's work on the Diaries of the Fourth Duke of Newcastle (Thoroton Record Series) is recommended reading, giving as it does the other side of the story of the early days of the Park's development. I have enjoyed talking about the Park with Allan Mulcahy, the author of the splendid *Conservation Plan for the Nottingham Park Estate* (2008). I am indebted to Maggie Hallam who first introduced me to The Park. Martine Hamilton Knight has been generous with the use of her photographs and I would like to thank the Park Estate Office for access to the Estate Map reproduced on the back cover.

All photographs, unless otherwise stated, are by the author.

Sources of reproduced documents are: N.U.M.D. University of Nottingham Manuscripts Department; N.A.O. Nottinghamshire Archives Office; L.S.L. Local Studies Library, Angel Row, Nottingham.

Hine Plaque, 19 Park Terrace

LIST OF ORIGINAL ESTATE HOUSES

(Houses built before 1914 and which continue to contribute positively to the character and appearance of the conservation area)

Albury Square: 5
Barrack Lane: 2, 10, 12, 14, 16, 18, 20, 22, 24, 26, 28, 30
Castle Grove: 4, 5, 6, 7
Cavendish Crescent North: 1, 3, 5, 7, 8, 9, 10, 11, 12, 14, 15, 16, 17, 18, 19, 20, 22, 24, Haddon House
Cavendish Crescent South: 1, 3, 5, 7, 9, 11, 13, 15, 17, 19, 21, 23, 25
Cavendish Road East: 23, 25, 27, 29, 31, 33 Cavendish House, Overdale, Elmhurst
Clare Valley: 1, 2, 3, 4, 5
Clifton Terrace: 1, 3, 4, Terrace House
Clumber Crescent North: 3, 5, 7, Clumber House
Clumber Crescent South: 5, 7
Clumber Road East: 3, Jelenice, Adam House, Edale House, Penryhn House
Clumber Road West: Linden House, Holly Lodge, Stowe House
Derby Road: 117, 119, 121, 123, 125, Clinton Terrace (1-7), Derby Terrace (1-9)
Duke William Mount: 1, 2, 3
Fiennes Crescent: The Coach House
Fishpond Drive: 4, 6, 30, 32
Hamilton Drive: la, lb, 1c, 2, 3, 4, 5, 6, 7, 8, 9, 10, 11, 24
Hardwick Road: Weston Lodge
Holles Crescent: 1, 3, 5
Hope Drive: 2, 4, 6, 8, 12, 14, 16, 18, 20, 22, 24, 26
Huntingdon Drive: 1, 2, 3, 4, 5, 6, 7, 8, 9, 10
Kenilworth Road: 1, 2, 3, 5
Lenton Avenue: 1, 3, 5, 7, 9, 11, 13, 15, 17, 19, 21, 23, 25, 27, 29, 31, 33
Lenton Road: 1, 2, 3, 4, 5, 6, 7, 7a, 8, 9, 11, 13, 13a, 15, 17, 19, 21, 23, 25, 27, 29, 31, 32, 33, 37, 43, 47
Lincoln Circus: Gladstone House
Newcastle Circus: 2, 7, Newcastle Court, Burton House, Castlethorpe
Newcastle Drive: 1, 3, 5, 7, 9, 11, 13, 15, 17, 19, 21, 23, 25, 27, 29, 31, 33, 35, 37, 39
North Road: 1, 2, 3, 5, 6, 7, 8
Park Drive: 1, 2, 3, 4, 6, 9, Ashley House
ParkTerrace: 1, 2, 3, 4, 5, 6, 7, 8, 9, 10, 11, 12, 14, 15, 16, 17, 18, 19, 20
Park Ravine: 2
Park Valley: 1, 3, 4, 5, 6, 7, 8, 9, 10, 11, 13, 15, 17, 19, 21, 23, 25
Pelham Crescent: 1, 3, 5, 7, 9, 10, 11, 13, 14, 15, 16, 17, 18, 19
Peveril Drive: 1, 2, 3, 6, 7, 8, 10, 11, 12, Peveril House
The Ropewalk: 2, 4, 6, 8, 10, 12, 14, 16, 18, 20, 22, 24, 26, 28, 30, 32, 34, 36, 38, 40, 42, 44, 48, 52, 54, 56
South Road: 1, 2, 3, 4, 5, 6
Tattershall Drive: 1, 2, 3, 4, 5
Western Terrace: 1, 2, 3, 4, 5, 6, 7, 8, 9, 10, 11

Compiled by Allan Mulcahy and reproduced with permission.

Track down these houses individually on the website: nottinghamparkhouses.co.uk